# The Road to Freedom

Taiwan's Postwar Human Rights Movement

本書是由財團法人臺灣民主基金會贊助出版。臺灣民主基金會是一個獨立、非營利的機構，其宗旨在促進臺灣以及全球民主、人權的研究與發展。臺灣民主基金會成立於二〇〇三年，是亞洲第一個國家級民主基金會，未來基金會志在與其他民主國家合作，促進全球新一波的民主化。

This book is published with the sponsorship of the Taiwan Foundation for Democracy (TFD). The TFD is an independent, non-profit foundation dedicated to the study and promotion of democracy and human rights in Taiwan and abroad. Founded in 2003, the TFD is the first democracy assistance foundation established in Asia. The Foundation is committed to the vision of working together with other democracies, to advance a new wave of democratization worldwide.

財團法人臺灣民主基金會
電話：+886-2-2708-0100，傳真：+886-2-2708-1128
電子郵件：tfd@taiwandemocracy.org.tw，網站：www.tfd.org.tw
For further information, please contact
Taiwan Foundation for Democracy:
(tel) +886-2-2708-0100, (fax) +886-2-2708-1128
(e-mail) tfd@taiwandemocracy.org.tw, (website) www.tfd.org.tw

# The Aesthetic of Violence

In 1990 I went to Chongqing, China, to see Zhazidong and Baigongguan, where Chiang Kai-shek carried out his political persecutions. In 1991, I went to Auschwitz and saw the concentration camp. The poison gas chambers into which the Nazis tricked their Jewish prisoners did not seem especially frightening after what I had already seen of the KMT legacy in China. At Zhazidong, I had seen something to make a person's hair stand on end: a club studded with nails. To be beaten with such a tool of torture would mean certain mutilation.

The most terrifying aspect of violence is the constant fear you feel when under its shadow. Those of us who lived through bullying and abuse at the hands of the Chiang family's secret police breathed a great sigh of relief when we were finally sentenced: it was like being finally able to lay down a heavy burden. It was not that we were happy to be alive but rather that our days were no longer a living death.

It sounds horrible to have one's fingernails torn off or nipples scalded, but what the secret police inflicted on your mind was worse. They took turns, piling humiliation upon insult twenty-four hours a day, to the point where your spirit went to pieces and you confessed, playing your part in the play they had scripted. What were your prayers, what did you beg for? To hurry up and die, because it just hurt so much.

However, the secret police were not about to give us any such satisfaction. All they had to do was put in two-hour shifts. We were allowed no time to rest. They would use threats or enticements on us, like the carrot and stick for the proverbial horse, in order to get us to "cough up" more names, so that an individual political case would expand to implicate potentially hundreds of people.

Every political prisoner is tortured by his conscience: either you submit to the pressure and cough up your "accomplices," or else you go down alone. Actually, heroes all turn into cowards once they are in prison. The Chiang family secret police had their blacklist, and they would kill a hundred innocents lest one guilty man should give them the slip. In the end, whether a prisoner confessed was simply a formality. The secret police would lie to the stalwarts, telling them that everyone else had already given in. No matter how tough you were, it was so painful to think you were the only one left. In the end you felt you had no other choice but give up and admit your "crime."

"Let me die!" was what all the political prisoners undergoing torture were saying to themselves. Living death, one's basic dignity trampled on, the thought of being betrayed by your comrades—what did death matter? The Daoist view that "Death is but a homecoming" was an empty slogan, because actually living through such misery was like being caught in a zone between life and death—you weren't really living, but they didn't let you die.

The sadness was even worse torture. You would catch glimpses through an iron grating that gave no daylight of comrades being dragged out of their cells and being taken to their executions. You felt left behind with a feeling of lifelong loneliness. It was not to know when spring would come, never to see the sun; it was not knowing if and when they would perform the "final inmate identity check" and send you walking down the road of no return.

A political prisoner must face ubiquitous violence. The jail in which he is detained is simply an enclosure. The world beyond the iron bars is more terrible still. Friends turn away. Facing incessant surveillance and intimidation, even kin may out of bitterness start to wonder, "Why did there have to be a political prisoner in my family?"

Once political prisoners are released, perhaps only their parents and wives are willing to take them in. If their children are not simply cold, they will at least resent their fathers for humiliating them for nothing. The day a political prisoner walks out of the prison gates is when he faces even greater shame and suffering.

During the thirty-eight years of martial law under the Kuomintang everyone regarded political prisoners as poisonous snakes and wild beasts. Anyone who associated with them was in for trouble. They were another kind; on their identity cards were special symbols only the secret police and personnel departments could decipher, such as the "forbidden from service" written in the military service column of my ID card. Finding a job was harder than scaling the sky.

Chiang Kai-shek and Chiang Ching-kuo held up political prisoners as chickens killed to scare the monkeys. They made an example of us in order to scare the resistance out of the Taiwanese people. But the executed no longer mattered. Sadder by far was the plight of the living. In 1982, when I was at Yuan-Liou Publishing Company compiling my *Dictionary of World History*, the deputy chief of Political Division Six came to my office every day, sat across from me, and kept me under close observation. This agent from the Taiwan Garrison Command kept this routine up for a hundred days straight! Since this book came out, Taiwanese publishing companies have avoided accepting my manuscripts, a prohibition that continues to this day! The two National Taiwan University students who proofread my work were almost expelled from school, and they would have been, had it not been for the courage of the late Professor Chang Chung-tung, who came forward to make an appeal on their behalf. The Bureau of Investigation "very generously" reduced their punishment to being held back for a year. It goes without saying that the *Dictionary of World History* is no longer in print.

According to the *Complete Statutes*, the complete collection of the laws of the Republic of China, political prisoners are to be deprived of over 38 different professional qualifications (for example, Article 3 of the Midwifery Act stipulates that "proven traitors of the Republic of China" cannot serve as midwives; credentials are to be revoked from practicing midwives).

I have never let such insults grind me down, because I am not the sort to sigh and complain that the world is not the way it should be. I would rather blame myself for not doing better. In the 25 years since my release, not once have I managed to find formal employment.

But though the government has done everything but kill me, I have kept my chin up. At the gate of the Auschwitz concentration camp, I saw a noose hanging from a gallows, which had been provided for the hanging of those responsible for the camp and now symbolized history's condemnation of the perpetrators of violence.

Those in power think that the fear of violence is enough for them to rule heaven and earth, but secretly their own hearts are full of fear. Violence is their opium, and the more they partake the more powerful their addiction. Nero got no satisfaction from throwing Christians to the lions because in the final analysis he was afraid, consumed by the fear that the victims would refuse to bow down their heads to him before dying.

Fear coils eternally around the hearts of perpetrators of violence. They find no peace in rest or repast, as an endless fear outlasts their transient explosions of violence. Violence is the method to which they become addicted, the opium they use to numb their fear. The more they perpetrate violence, the more afraid they become.

On March 29, 2002, 25 years after my release, I returned to Green Island, also commonly known as "Burnt Island." I saw the now-dilapidated political prison, my second home in this life. What I saw there was not the place that had swallowed my youth but rather the sad and pathetic faces of Chiang Kai-shek and Chiang Ching-kuo. I could almost catch a glimpse of the vain specters of the powerful and mighty flitting about in the hollow and deserted spaces.

Where today is state violence used to subdue the defenseless citizen, native Taiwanese and Mainlander alike? Where today do we see rulers subduing Taiwan with brute force? Chiang the Father and Chiang the Son and their secret police never dreamed the judgment of history would come so quickly.

The dialogue between the perpetrators and the victims of violence begins and ends with violence. Of this history bears witness. The present generation is overly lenient and all-too forgiving. Far be it from them to repay the perpetrators of violence with a taste of their own medicine. But even unpunished, the hearts of the perpetrators of violence are forever consumed by fear.

There was a rumor spread through the Mainlander communities that if the day came when the native Taiwanese stood up and took control, they would toss the "foreigners" into the sea to feed the sharks. It turns out that this rumor was fabricated by the secret police, who wanted to generate fear among the Mainlanders to keep them solidly behind the KMT. The psychology that drove these perpetrators of violence to tell such lies has condemned them to drift eternally in an abyss of apprehension.

What do I mean by the "aesthetic of violence?" I mean that moment when the perpetrators of violence spontaneously lay down their weapons because they are suddenly powerless in the presence of their victims. We political prisoners have suffered the tortures of a man-made purgatory, and yet here we are, still smiling, ironically mocking all who use violence against their fellow human beings.

Today, the sunshine of freedom has breached the clouds; martial law has lifted. A haze may still hang in the sky over Taiwan, but at least we no longer have institutionalized violence. The sacrifice of the innumerable political prisoners who have shed their blood since the February 28 Incident has not been in vain. 24 years ago, my wife and I chose the theme from the 1960 movie Exodus as our wedding march:

*And when the morning sun reveals her hills and plain*
*Then I see a land where children can run free.*

The smiles on the children's faces and the bright future they see when they look up to the sky tell me that my people have crossed the desert and found the Promised Land.

Nothing more than an ordinary Taiwanese political prisoner, I've been so lucky because in the end I won far more applause than those who used violence against me; the greatest pride for us political prisoners is our commitment to justice. Violence was once used to oppress us, but we did not yield.

My only hope is that we victims of violence will become its witnesses, so that the next generation will remember and live with dignity.

## About the Author

*Yang Pi-chuan (1949~) is from Hsinchu. His father spent more than a decade in political prison. His mother died of grief. After graduating from high school, he formed an organization with a group of young men who wanted to overthrow the government of the Republic of China. He was caught in 1970 and spent seven years in prison. He is widely read and has written voluminously. He now devotes himself to writing and academic research.*

# The Soul's Long Night

The last decade of the 20th century was a tumultuous one for Taiwan. Chiang Ching-kuo, the last of the Chiang family to rule the country, had died in 1988, setting the stage for the democratic transformation of the 1990s. Not only did all the parliamentarians come to be chosen by popular election, but also the president. The first presidential election was held in 1996. In the second presidential election, held in the year 2000, Taiwan experienced its first-ever democratic political succession, as the Kuomintang was defeated by Chen Shui-bian's Democratic Progressive Party. Another achievement of which we may be proud is that many human rights and freedoms were given legal guarantee over the course of the decade. This impressive progress has won Taiwan recognition and affirmation around the world.

The American human rights organization Freedom House conducts an annual survey to classify the nations of the world into three categories according to the level of freedom enjoyed by citizens. These three categories are free, partly free, and not free. Since the year 2000, Taiwan has been listed as a free nation, in the same class as the UK, Japan, France, and Germany. Our neighbor on the other side of the straits, which calls itself a People's Republic, was ranked second from the bottom among the "not free" nations, in the same class as Ruanda and Cameroon. Democratic Taiwan and totalitarian China now present a stark contrast of political systems.

Taiwan's growth into a tall tree in the forest of democratic nations did not happen overnight. The rights and freedoms the people of Taiwan now enjoy were won through a long, long period of struggle. This is a history written in blood, sweat and tears. We do not know how many people died in a blood exchange for the democratic liberties we now enjoy. We do not know how many heroes gave their lives in sacrifice, how many families were broken, how much happiness was lost, or how many promising youths were cut off, like unripe fruits plucked from the tree of life.

We must not forget the hardships we have faced and the bitterness we have had to swallow. Before we can properly treasure the present, we need to understand the past. Before we can be truly ready to greet the day, we must come to know the darkest hours of the night.

In the wake of the Second World War, the Kuomintang arrived from the mainland to take control of Taiwan. The people living on the island initially greeted the newcomers with open arms, not realizing that the new regime wanted to conquer and subdue Taiwan, not to "liberate" it. Taiwan immediately faced a host of crises: political corruption, the abuse of privilege, an economic slump, a sharp drop in production, food shortages, uncontrollable inflation, a steep jump in unemployment, the failure of military discipline, bandits running wild, and a degeneration in public order. Trampled on for a short sixteen months, Taiwanese social development was pushed back by three or four decades. Social discontent was intense; Taiwan was a powderkeg. Then, in 1947, the February 28 Incident was sparked.

During the incident, Taiwan's citizens stood up to demand democratic reforms, in response to which Chiang Kai-shek sent troops from the mainland to quash these "opponents" to his rule. The suppression turned into a massacre, which was followed by an island-wide manhunt for political opponents. The people suffered heavy casualties in what was called a "Countrywide Sweep." Untold numbers of the brightest lights of the newest generation made the greatest sacrifice. Both socially and politically, the February 28 Incident has had a massive impact on Taiwan still felt today.

About two and a half years after the February 28 Incident, Chiang Kai-shek's Kuomintang regime retreated after its defeat to the communists and established a "settler state" on Taiwan. The wounds the people had suffered during the February 28 Incident had not yet healed, and now salt was to be rubbed in with the onset of the age of White Terror politics.

From the Korean War in the early 1950s to the worsening situation in Vietnam during the 1960s, international politics became polarized. In this geopolitical state of affairs, Taiwan had immense strategic importance for the United States. With US bolstering, it was natural for the Chiang regime to adopt a policy of resistance to Chinese and Russian communism.

A political myth was invented to support both this policy and the government's very right to rule. On the face of it, the myth seemed reasonable: Chiang Kai-shek was the legitimate leader of the Chinese people, but by great misfortune China had been usurped by the communists, who brought unimaginable suffering to the people. Furthermore, in the process of building party and state, the communists had received plenty of support from the Soviet Union and, as the "willing

lackeys of Soviet imperialism," were thus traitors to the Chinese people. In the face of this outrage, the people of Taiwan had to do something. They needed to rescue their compatriots from communism, and to accomplish this required that they "serve with unswerving loyalty, weed out the communist spies, and overthrow the Russian bandits."

Briefly, in the first decades of the Chiang regime on Taiwan, nationalism, ethnic pride, and Chiang Kai-shek's personal ideology of heroism were thrown into the pot to mix a potent and intoxicating brew. As this myth was the theoretical foundation of Chiang Kai-shek's political power, he brooked no challenge to it. Whoever was dubious of this sacred "basic policy of state" was automatically a "communist spy" or a "communist propagandist." Out of nationalism and ethnic pride, everybody was obligated to aid in the exposure and elimination of the communist spies, who were supposedly rife among us.

Historically, any regime that lacks a sense of security uses high-pressure tactics to purge the people it considers to be its opponents. Dissidents have to be punished in order to scare opposition out of the rest of the populace. To build a firm foundation for his rule of Taiwan, Chiang Kai-shek made use of two mutually explicating and reinforcing pieces of legislation, the Martial Law and the Temporary Provisions Effective During the Period of Communist Rebellion.

Chiang Kai-shek was still on the mainland on May 19, 1949, when the CCP's revolution blew up in his face. The governor of Taiwan at the time was Chen Cheng. Without consulting any higher power, Chen Cheng announced that Martial Law was in effect starting on the morning of May 20, even though there was no unrest in the country whatsoever.

Chiang Kai-shek arrived battered and beaten six months later. Martial Law was not revoked. The people's basic rights and freedoms, such as freedom of assembly, association, speech, and publication were sharply curtailed, a ban was placed on the establishment of new political parties, and travel abroad was tightly restricted. Martial Law was sustained for a world-record 38 years until 1987.

The Temporary Provisions Effective During the Period of Communist Rebellion were promulgated on May 9, 1948, when the Chiang regime was still in Nanking. The Constitution of the Republic of China was not five months old, and now these unconstitutional regulations were added to it. They were supposedly to increase the president' s authority to undertake emergency disciplinary measures, but their actual purpose was to increase Chiang Kai-shek's personal power. On this legal basis, there was no limit to the number of terms of office Chiang Kai-shek and his son Chiang Ching-kuo could serve, effectively giving them control over the Executive Yuan, according to the Constitution the highest executive body. Revised many times, these "temporary" regulations were not finally abolished until 1991.

The Martial Law and the Temporary Provisions were not the only tricks up their sleeves. Emphasizing the need to "suppress the rebellion," Chiang regime brought back old pieces of laws and regulations lying around from the Sino-Japanese War and the Civil War. Chiang applied this outmoded legislation, either without any amendment or with an increase in severity. Chiang also developed new weapons to use against dissidents, wickedly harsh legislation such as the Statutes for the Detection and Eradication of Spies During the Period of Communist Rebellion.

Naturally, governance based on martial law and a legal system for the suppression of rebellion required an intricate network of secret police for enforcement. Set up in 1949, the Political Action Committee became the government organ for eliminating communists and dissidents of any other stripe. In July 1949, Chiang Kai-shek began paving the road to power for his elder son, Chiang Ching-kuo, starting with the secret police network and continuing with the party, the government and the military. In the middle of the 1950s, he also established the National Security Bureau to centralize command of the various organs of intelligence such as the Taiwan Garrison Command, the Bureau of Investigation, and the Intelligence Bureau.

This web-like secret police force caught the people of Taiwan in a new White Terror era. Under the pretext of "eliminating communist spies," many who had opposing political views or who dared criticize the government were rounded up and executed on trumped-up charges. Below is an overview of the major types of political case that occurred during the White Terror.

1. Strikes at left-wing movements sympathetic to Chinese communism, such as the 1949 Keelung Work Committee Case, in which Chung Hao-tung and others were involved *(see page 35)*, the 1950 Taipei Work Committee Case *(page 34)*, and the 1952 Luku Base Case *(page 35)*.

2. Purges of the Taiwan independence movement and its proponents, such as the 1950 and 1962 Taiwan independence cases involving Thomas Wen-yi Liao *(see page 36)*, the Chen Chih-Hsiung Case in 1962 *(page 86)*, and the 1967 National Youth Solidarity Promotion Association Case *(page 34)*.

3. Purges directed at the Aboriginal self-rule movement, which involved the murders of Leshin Wadan, Kao Yi-sheng, Tang Shou-jen, and other Indigenous talents *(see page 37)*.

4. Moves to crush the democracy movement, such as the fabricated Lei Chen Case, which caused a nascent opposition party just in the process of organizing to be stillborn *(see page 109)*.

5. Cases arising out of political struggles, such as the fabricated Sun Li-jen Case, in which General Sun's military authority was repudiated *(see page 39)*.

6. Cases arising out of internal secret police struggles, such as the Chiang Hai-jung and Li Shih-chieh Case, both of them high-level Bureau of Investigation directors *(see page 40)*.

7. Literary inquisition cases, which incarcerated Po Yang, Lee Ao, Chen Ying-chen, and other writers.

8. The uncountable number of feigned cases fabricated by the secret police in order to win prizes and inflate their performance record.

Similar cases can be ennumerated endlessly.

They were all the natural outcome of the system set up by the Chiang family to control the country and establish their dynasty.

A society that does not know its own history is blind and ignorant. A people that forgets its history easily is heartless and unjust. There is no way for such a people and society to achieve the long period of political stability characteristic of a truly modern nation. The book you hold in your hands is a record of those dark times. Though its tales of blood and tears will make your heart ache, in the course of reading you will become more able to treasure a present that did not come easily. You will also be readied to march towards a future filled with promise and hope.

* The author is professor of Taiwanese history at Shih Hsin University.

# Indomitable Spirits

P ublished in 2002, the original, Chinese, version of *The Road to Freedom: Retrospective on Taiwan's Democratic Struggle and Human Rights Movement* was a compilation that included and supplemented materials displayed in an exhibit on democracy and human rights held, ironically and yet appropriately, in the first floor gallery of the Presidential Building in December 2001. The exhibit and book were milestones in research on the important themes of democracy and human rights. With much material having come to light in the three years since then, this book is a revision as much as it is a translation. And behind it all, in charge of planning and execution, was the Dr Chen Wen-chen Memorial Foundation.

Chen Wen-chen was born in 1950 in Taipei County. He graduated from National Taiwan University with a degree in mathematics, and went to America to continue his studies at the University of Michigan. Upon the completion of his PhD, he began teaching at Carnegie Mellon University in Pittsburgh and doing theoretical research in statistics, which came to be highly esteemed internationally by his fellow mathematicians. Though abroad, he remained concerned about developments in his home country, especially in the human rights movement, of which he was an ardent supporter. In the summer of 1981, he went home to see his relatives, but the visit was interrupted by the secret police when he was taken to the Taiwan Garrison Command on July 2 for questioning. The next day, his corpse turned up on the campus of his alma mater. In those fateful days, your only reward if you took action to demonstrate your love of Taiwan was punishment by the authorities. And so Chen paid with his life.

And yet, Professor Chen's sacrifice heralded the end of the White Terror. His death has had a catalytic effect on Taiwan's democratic and human rights movements. For the past 23 years, his indomitable spirit has lit the way like a lamp, shining brilliantly on the land he loved and passing on the flame.

The incident spurred many to speak out against the government and organize activities that brought the facts to light. They picked the lock the KMT had placed on information and began reporting and following up on the homicide. Their next step was to get the word out through public lectures or in writing, in order to awaken international concern about the issue of human rights in Taiwan. Taiwanese living abroad wore masks while demonstrating, for fear that KMT spies might report on them for a repeat of the Chen tragedy. They also gave testimony at US Congressional hearings, voicing their demand for the truth in this case. We can still hear their voices today, as the case remains unsolved. This was almost certainly a case of accidental death by torture or a first-degree political murder, but almost a quarter of a century later the killers and the masterminds have not been brought to justice.

For this same period of time, events memorializing Chen have gone on without interruption, though the activities themselves have changed. We began by investigating the truth of what happened, and moved on to the theme of the end of political persecution, seeking to promote human rights concerns, ethnic tolerance and critical cultural reflection, while continuing to share the inspiration of Chen's idealist spirit.

One activity in memory of Chen was the establishment of this foundation. We have put out publications, presented exhibits, and organized lectures and academic symposia. We have also set up a Chen Wen-chen scholarship to celebrate and bequeath Chen's spiritual gift to posterity. At different stages, we choose different ways of paying our respects to this champion of the cause of human rights, but though the forms may differ the motivating spirit of love remains the same. It is this love for Taiwan that Chen has shared with us.

We held four "Island Melody" concerts in Chen's memory in 1992, 1994, 1995, 1997. In July 2001, the premiere of *Ilha Formosa—Requiem for Martyr of Formosa* was performed at the National Concert Hall, on the twentieth anniversary of Chen's death. The piece was composed by Tyzen Hsiao, with lyrics by the poet Lee Min-yung. In 1993, 1995, 1997 and 1999, we held four traveling photographic exhibits, entitled "Images of Our Island Nation" and organized around Taiwanese historical figures. Each of these traveling exhibits was followed by the publication of a book. The publication of *The Road to Freedom* in its Chinese and English versions continues our effort to awaken awareness about Taiwanese history and to remember with gratitude Chen's vital patriotism. In 1996, we found another way to pay tribute to this human rights warrior: the Taiwan Human Rights Film Festival, another nation-wide traveling enterprise.

These activities were conducted as consolation and cleansing rituals for the spirits of countless victims, and they represent an effort to unveil and correct a history that has been warped and buried. These activities are also intended to light the way by making us more attentive and even vigilant in the face of a highly uncertain future.

A1

December 2001 exhibition "The Road to Freedom " opens at Presidential Building.

Thanks go to all the personnel involved and to all who have provided information. I cannot express how grateful I am to you for making all of this possible.

*\*Shen Yi-fang is chairman of the Dr. Chen Wen-chen Memorial Foundation.*

# Contents

## ■ White Terror

## ■ Road to Freedom

*Although Tongyong has been adopted as the official romanization system in Taiwan, we have used Wade-Giles for romanization of names since this was the system in use during the period covered by the book.*

## ■ Human Rights Rescue

## ■ Human Rights Prospect

*Sources of the graphic materials may be learned by referencing the index number appearing beside the graphic in the list of credits on pp. 172-3. We would like to thank everyone who generously supplied these graphic materials.*

# Human Rights in Postwar Taiwan

**Crushingly defeated in the Pacific War and shocked by Hiroshima and Nagasaki, on August 15, 1945 Japan announced its final surrender. Her empire had stretched over a fifth of the world's surface, but now all of that was gone, including her very first colony, Taiwan, which China (the Qing Dynasty) had ceded to Japan in 1895 as a spoil of war. Called "Ilha Formosa," or "Beautiful Island," by the Europeans, Taiwan had known three centuries of imperial domination. Japan was its fourth conqueror, following in the footsteps of Holland, Spain, and China.**

On October 25, 1945, a Japanese representative stood in the Taipei Public Assembly Hall and surrendered to Chen Yi, representing Generalissimo Chiang Kai-shek, the Allied Forces' supreme commander in the Chinese Theater. This transfer ceremony has been misinterpreted ever since by both regimes—by the Chinese Nationalist Party (Kuomintang, KMT) and by its rival, the Chinese Communist Party (CCP)—as being a case of "Taiwan's return to the motherland." Of course, each side regarded itself as the true motherland. In the nearly sixty years since the end of the Second World War, Taiwan has paid an extremely high price for this distorted interpretation of history.

Led by Chiang Kai-shek, the KMT regime declared this "motherland" was the KMT's own Republic of China. Once Taiwan came under their control, there were three dramatic periods of encounter between the mainland regime and the local Taiwanese people. Each of these periods had a deep impact on Taiwanese politics and society.

The first such encounter began in October 1945 with the arrival from China of the officials, troops, and secret police under Governor Chen Yi, to take over the reins of power from the Japanese. They were warmly welcomed by the people of Taiwan—unaware that the corrupt old Chen Yi would soon plunge the nation into an unprecedented economic and social crisis. Less than two years later, on February 28, 1947, a popular island-wide resistance rose up to fight the oppressors.

The second period started when Chiang Kai-shek responded to his governor's request for a division to come to Taiwan to crush the resistance. The troops arrived at Keelung on March 9, 1947, marking the beginning of a bloody campaign called the "Countrywide Sweep." The massacre lasted until the middle of May.

In 1949, at the end of the Chinese civil war, the KMT, soundly defeated by Mao Zedong's CCP, fled to Taiwan with two million refugees including an army that they claimed to number six hundred thousand. During this third period of contact, the KMT used high-pressure tactics to bring to heel the six million people of Taiwan, who enormously outnumbered the Mainlanders. This was the beginning of the forty years of White Terror.

In Taiwan's postwar history, the February 28 Incident and the White Terror have caused the greatest harm to the cause of human rights. According to conservative estimates, in the February 28 Incident alone, twenty to thirty thousand persons were executed without trial or any sort of judicial proceeding. Yet that number does not do true justice to the enormity of the tragedy, in which KMT troops kidnapped, raped, ransomed, robbed, and murdered— or even indiscriminately massacred—untold numbers of their own citizens. It was as if they were invading an enemy state, or governing a foreign colony.

In December 1951, a young left-wing prisoner named Fu Wei-liang asked someone to paint this so that he could send it to his daughter. Several days later, before it was even Christmas, Fu was taken out and executed. He was only 25.

The way the massacre was carried out reminds one of the 1937 Nanjing Massacre in China or of the "ethnic cleansing" that occurred in the 1990s in the former Yugoslavia. There was something particularly sick and abusive to it. According to a great deal of historical evidence and eyewitness accounts, many of the dead had had their noses, ears, and genitals hacked off; many had had their hands and feet pierced by iron wire; many had been beaten to death or drowned in the ocean. Trucks of corpses shuttled down streets wet with blood, depositing their freight into rivers that ran crimson, or into the vast and silent sea. This was a vast slaughterhouse. This was hell on earth.

And yet the above account does not adequately convey that hell's full measure. There were more,

many more, who simply disappeared. According to eyewitnesses, during the Incident, soldiers would go door to door, arresting every young man they found. Once taken away, these young men were never heard from again. Their families were consequently plunged into the torture of endless worry. A certificate of death would have ended part of their misery, but none was given. Their sons, brothers, husbands, and fathers had gone permanently "missing." So many years later, when various construction projects started unearthing their decomposed remains, none of them have finally, at long last, become identifiable. As for the dead, who can say who they were, and who is dreaming of them still?

The February 28 Incident frightened the people of Taiwan to death, leaving their hearts twisted with apprehension and the pain of loss. Another form of inflicted hurt was the sacrifice of the local socio-political elite. With the elite eliminated, the way was now clear for the KMT's full takeover of all domestic resources on its path to becoming the compleat settler-state regime.

When the KMT came to Taiwan in 1949, the people of Taiwan did not, as they had four years earlier, welcome them with open arms. In fact, certain members of the social and intellectual elite who had survived the February 28 Incident began planning revenge. Inspired by an idealistic socialist philosophy and excited by the KMT's defeat at the hands of the communists, they banded together under the flag of the Taiwan Provincial Work Committee, an underground organization directed by the CCP. This organization's membership grew from less than ninety in March 1947 to over nine hundred in May 1950, when it was busted.

Many in the leadership ranks of the TPWC gave themselves up to the KMT and even provided detailed intelligence, which led to the collapse of the organization within the space of only a few months. The authorities also used the information they obtained to arrest and murder many left-wing intellectuals. But these people represented only a small portion of the victims of the White Terror.

The startling fact is that most of the victims were innocent. Even more shocking is the number of people persecuted: at least a hundred times the number who joined the communist party. Former parliamentarian

Hsieh Tsung-min has reported that he was informed by a high-level official that over 90 thousand people, both military and civilian, were arrested on charges of rebellion, which means an average of six sedition arrests per day.

As to the number executed, that is as hard to ascertain as is the number killed during the February 28 Incident. In both cases, the number of missing persons is huge. According to conservative estimates, around three thousand were given the death sentence, but in addition to the cases that were administered formally, there was a greater number where secret executions followed upon star-chamber justice. This continued at least until the 1970s. We have every reason to believe that three thousand is only the tip of the iceberg.

One statistic stands out. In May 1960, the director of the Martial Law Section of the Taiwan Garrison Command indicated in a report to the Taiwan Provincial Assembly that over the years there were 126,875 people in Taiwan whose status was "whereabouts unknown." This being Taiwan of the 1950s, an intricate police and secret police network was in place to enforce Martial Law. Travel abroad was tightly restricted. In this context, it boggles the mind to imagine how over a hundred and twenty thousand individuals could go missing on an island eleven times smaller than California. The only reasonable explanation is that the overwhelming majority had either been long-term fugitives or else had been arrested or executed in secret, just as occurred during the February 28 Incident.

Two young secret agents sent by the Security Command to watch *Free China*'s offices were surreptitiously photographed by someone inside in June 1951. The foremost political review of the fifties was banned in 1960.

B4

A group of young victims of the White Terror from Tainan: Ting Yao-tiao, *back row center*, and her friends. The three National Taiwan University students *in the front row* are, *from left*, Chang Tsang-han (seven years' imprisonment), Wu Tung-lieh (dead), and Shih Chih-chen (went underground). *Back row left*, Shih Chih-chen's older sister, Shih Shui-huan (dead).

B5

At the time of her execution in 1956, Ting Yao-tiao had her infant in prison with her. When the time of her execution drew nigh, the infant was torn from her breast and Ting was led to the execution ground, *top*, and was shot, *bottom*. A half-century later her comrade-in-arms Kuo Chen-chun *(see p.49)* finally procured copies of these black and white photos from recently declassified files, and was able to create this montage in her memory.

B6

A group of prisoners on Green Island, forced to do hard labor under conditions of tight security.

B7

An old and sick National Assembly member, not once reelected in over forty years, carries his external bladder.

Shocking as these facts about the missing are, the true casualty figure for the White Terror is even higher. The one hundred and twenty thousand-plus individuals mentioned above only account for the portion of the population that had already registered—which didn't include the many mainland refugees in Taiwan in the late 1940s and early 50s. Many of them were killed in secret before they had a chance to register, and many were tossed into the sea before they even set foot on Taiwanese ground. In wartime, life was cheap, and the lives of refugees were worth about as much as bugs crushed under some colonel's boot. In sum, we will never know how many died during their escape to Taiwan.

The KMT rooted out the local social elite and sentenced many innocents to death, leaving the survivors too scared to speak out. This foreign military regime maintained the world's longest period of martial law. They turned Taiwan into a human rights wasteland and a despot's pleasure-park. Taiwan could not be allowed to develop into a normal state, because this would compromise the KMT's illegal rule.

The KMT claimed that since its enemy, the Chinese Communist Party, tyrannized desperate and suffering millions, the people of Taiwan bore a sacred mission, embodied in the slogan, "Counterattack the Mainland and Rescue our Compatriots!" As a result, Taiwan endured many years of militarization, which shot military expenditures into the stratosphere. For a long time, military spending represented over 50 percent of the central government's budget. These were strange times, during which Taiwan was mobilized for war against China and the government was ready to suppress any resistance from the local populace. The KMT did not see the people of Taiwan as their "own people." Taiwan was simply a springboard for counterattack, of no importance in itself. Nor could she be allowed to exchange her military uniform for the modern garb of democracy.

Under martial law, the people of Taiwan were supposed to both believe in this myth of the necessity of taking back the mainland and accept the consequent need for a policy of pared-down democracy, liberty and human rights. Any dissent was sure to evoke ringing accusations of "spying for the communists" or "rebellion."

In order to handle the communist spies, whom the authorities claimed were hiding everywhere, an anachronistic system from imperial times was imposed on teachers and civil servants. In this system, mere association with someone judged guilty of an offense made you liable for punishment. Numbering in the hundreds of thousands, the police, secret police and informers turned Taiwan into a police state and caught the people in an invisible web of surveillance. There was an intricate system of draconian legislation, but often the Chiang regime did not even bother with the regular legislative channels, because administrative orders could simply be funneled through the secret police, which handled their promulgation and enforcement. In this way, all executive measures, however illegal, were made legal. Military rule was not simply legitimated but also indoctrinated—the military ethos infiltrated the schools, and education became the inculcation of the official ideology. Taiwan was now the perfect model of a fascist state.

This state was thus: a body of people numbering no more than ten million in the 1950 supplied and supported a government apparatus large enough to govern a nation of six hundred million. This apparatus calling itself the "legitimate government of China" had all the trappings of a giant power, with two thousand parliamentarians claiming to represent the will of their constituents in what had in the meantime become the People's Republic of China, in the People's Republic of Mongolia, and in Tibet.

The secret police were the most notorious component in the White Terror machine. Through long practice many secret police became expert at plainclothes surveillance, mail inspection, and telephone monitoring, while others specialized in the arts of torture, fabrication of facts, and trumped-up accusations. They would do whatever it took to send an innocent man to prison or to death. All they needed was "proof" that he was the perpetrator of a crime he'd never committed or the member of an organization he'd never even heard of. And anyone could be "proven" guilty.

Behind these nefarious secret police activities, which won death sentences for legions of political prisoners, there was an economic motivation—a motivation driven by a system of promotions and economic incentives. The rewards were funded by property confiscated from prisoners sentenced to death or given long prison sentences. The government would reserve a portion of the confiscated resources to "personnel who had rendered great service in handling the case." Thus, robbery and murder were carried out in the name of the nation. Base crimes were made into symbols of justice. The 1952 Luku Case is an example: Chiang Kai-shek issued 1.2 million dollars in prize money. To win twenty thousand (equivalent to a hundred months' salary for an ordinary civil servant) you needed to "produce" one death sentence, and to win ten thousand you needed to put someone away for a decade. As one might imagine, there was a frenzy of torture to extract confessions.

At that time Taiwan had a very special form of government. Chiang Ching-kuo had learned various techniques from the Russians, such as how to impose a "political cadre" system on the military, the government and the schools, on top of which there were also the dictatorship, the thought police, and various institutions designed to maintain his despotic rule. Further, the corruption and "rule of the few" that gave rise to the February 28 Incident were already built into the system well before that tragic affair.

Naturally, all of this was varnished over. The mainstream media, the KMT's mouthpiece, would repeat that all was well no matter what was going on. It was ridiculed by the people, who said that you had to watch it "upside down" to know what was really going on. And, as for the judicial system, in a democracy the last line of defense for human rights, people in Taiwan used to say that the courts were run by the KMT as a business.

These appalling deeds and injustices did not see the light of day until they began to be revealed in the late 1980s. But even today, only a small part of the truth has been made public. Still, this is an opportunity to celebrate a small victory in the struggle for human rights in Taiwan, as it has cost a third of a century of hard struggle just to be able to take up these matters publicly.

The martial law system that the KMT used to carry out the White Terror was solid as a rock, so bringing it down proved to be a difficult and time-consuming task. From the 1950s through the end of the 1970s, democratic activists could play a limited watchdog role by running independent magazines and participating in local elections, yet they had very

far to go before there would be a system of checks and balances.

The authorities often thwarted their democratic activities, however, by suspending their publications or banning their magazines outright. As election candidates, they had to win by overwhelming margins to make it impossible for the KMT to rig the ballots and steal victory from the real winner—situations like "sudden" power outages during the ballot count, with a switching of ballot boxes before power could be restored. The KMT also could, and often did, choose the more expensive route of vote-buying to ensure a huge electoral majority. Using such tactics to gain advantage, the KMT only hastened the corruption of Taiwan's political culture.

Beginning in the mid-seventies, a series of open protests against such election fraud culminated in the Chungli Incident of 1977, in which the devil of Martial Law faced very serious challenge for the first time. The demonstration ended in bloodshed, but resulted in a series of activities through which the power of the people pressured the authorities for change. It was prologue to a milestone in the democratic human rights movement—the 1979 Kaohsiung Incident, which involved a raid on the reformist *Formosa Monthly* magazine. Although democratic activists faced another onslaught of mass arrests in 1979-80, this setback only served to goad the movement to a stronger sense of consensus and common strength. In the 1980s, in numberless street marches, volleys were launched at the despotic regime and at every part of the martial law system.

The uproar of the people left Chiang Ching-kuo with no choice but to lift martial law in 1987. The Democratic Progressive Party, formally established the previous year, brought party politics onto the historical agenda. After the death of Chiang Ching-kuo in 1988, Lee Teng-hui succeeded to the office and became the first native Taiwanese president. Reelected twice, he served from 1988 to 2000. Together Lee and the DPP hastened democratization. During this time, conservatives often tried to use their influence to resist the changes, but comprehensive political reform had become an unstoppable trend.

At the time, the international environment was changing radically. The Cold War thawed, the Soviet Union fragmented, and it was spring at last for the

Standing proudly smack in front of the Chiang Kai-shek Memorial Hall
was this "Taiwan lily", a symbol of the spirit of the student movement.

nations of Eastern Europe, giving rise to the hope that the world had come into a vast and powerful magnetic field of reconciliation. In these new times, it seemed absurd for Taiwan to continue Martial Law. From the 1970s, Taiwan had been counted among Asia's four sunrise industry nations, the "four little dragons." This was a time of rapid accumulation of wealth. By the 1990s, Taiwan had become one of the world's economic powers. The people were now relatively well off, with confidence and resources enough to go into politics or social reconstruction and to exert themselves for the well-being of the homeland.

At the dawn of the 21st century, the fourteen-year-old DPP finally, in Taiwan's first-ever democratic political succession, brought an end to a half-century of KMT rule. The DPP was reelected in 2004. Since 1988, Taiwan has entered a new period, in which locally born Taiwanese have finally taken charge of the country. This was when Taiwan-consciousness replaced China-consciousness—in other words, a crucial stage in the reformulation of national identity.

National identity is a thorny problem, especially in Taiwan. The KMT planted the dubious notion that "there is only one China and Taiwan is part of it" in the social subconscious, where it grew into a conviction. The CCP uses this same proposition to claim sovereignty over Taiwan and justify its strategy of shutting Taiwan out of the international arena.

Having been threatened by Holland, Spain, the Qing Dynasty, Japan, and the KMT, Taiwan now faces a sixth regime with designs upon it: communist China. The CCP continues to hold the tyrannical posture that it has a historic right to rule Taiwan. A foreign power with a "right to rule!" This pernicious notion, which fated Taiwan to four hundred years of tragedy, is not yet dead. It represents the most important factor affecting whether Taiwan's democratic human rights can be protected in the long run.

However, at least on Taiwanese soil the flowers of democratic human rights are blooming. It has taken a long time to attend to the examination of history, the investigation of truth, and the redress of wrongs committed against political victims. But better late than never! There has been staunch opposition domestically and abroad to building Taiwan into a politically normal country, a task that takes an enormous amount of energy under even the best of conditions. But the will to make it happen has now gone mainstream.

In the Taiwanese language, the pronunciation of "Taiwan" sounds a lot like "burying the misfortune," a phrase that reminds one of the dark side of much of Taiwan's history, a story of suffering. But "Taiwan" also sounds very similar to "big wishing," which seems to promise that the dark times are done and a bright future lies ahead.

# A Human Rights Chrono

▶ **September 10, 1973**
## Universities Police Long Hair and 'Strange Apparel'

Off-campus fashions are not exempt. On February 5, 1972, the Chengchung Precinct of the Taipei police mobilizes all their forces, nabbing 450 long-haired males, 67 with bell-bottom pants, and thirteen females in mini-skirts.

▶ **February 22, 1974**
## Taipei City Polices Sixteen Christian Colleges

Deprivation of such civil freedoms as the right to establish new schools.

▶ **January 1975**
## Hoklo-Language Bibles Banned

Policing activity of this sort traceable back to 1953. With Mandarin being promoted in the 1970s, and in order to strike at the Presbyterian Church in Taiwan, banning activities become all the more energetic.

▶ **April 5, 1975**
## Chiang Kai-shek Dies

On May 30, the Legislative Yuan passes the Statutes for Reduction of Sentence, allowing the release of 7000 prisoners, with less than 200 political prisoners winning reduction of sentence, resulting in release for roughly half of them.

▶ **January 8, 1976**
## Broadcast and Television Law Implemented

Stipulating that Mandarin should be the main language used for broadcast, it calls for the gradual reduction of "dialects."

▶ **August 1977**
## Native Literature Debate

Anti-communist literature versus native literature. From July 15 to November 24, officialdom and two big newspapers publish 58 articles attacking native literature, rousing the native literature writers to counterattack. The curtain falls on the polemic in January 1978, and concern for native issues takes root thereafter.

▶ **August 16, 1977**
## Presbyterian Church in Taiwan Issues 'A Declaration on Human Rights'

The PCT calls for Taiwan to become "a new and independent country."

▶ **January 1, 1979**
## US and Taiwan Break Official Ties

With KMT loss of American support, more and more peopl become concerned about Taiwan's future.

▶ **December 10, 1979**
## Kaohsiung Incident

Described by international human rights groups as a "polic riot," this is a seminal event in the history of Taiwan's democrati movement. *See p. 118.*

▶ **July 1, 1981**
## National Compensation Law Promulgated

Should citizens be harmed by the conduct of government officials they can now demand compensation. Political offenders are excluded.

▶ **August 26, 1982**
## Policing of New Testament Church

The home of the church on Mt. Zion in Kaohsiung County i demolished, and its adherents forced down off the mountair with some of them sentenced. After this, church followers becom among the most active of street demonstrators.

▶ **November 12, 1984**
## Sweep of Gangs: The Yiching Campaign

In the wake of Henry Liu's murder in October 1984, over tw thousand people are arrested by September 1985. The Yichin; Campaign targets not only gangsters: many social movemen activists and Tangwai supporters are taken in as well.

▶ **December 29, 1984**
## Taiwan Association for Promotion of Aboriginal Rights Established

The largest of Indigenous movement organizations demand that the descendants of Taiwan's earliest inhabitants be called b their tribal (which is to say non-Chinese) names, and that they b allowed self-rule. They also launch three marches as part of th "give us back our land" movement. Whereas in the past, use o Han names was forced on them, Aborigines are allowed to rever to use of their original names, thanks to legislation passed by th Legislative Yuan in 1995.

▶ **March 1, 1985**
## Labor Standards Law Goes into Effect

First applied only to the manufacturing sector, in December 199 it comes to cover "every for-hire relationship."

## June 17, 1998
### Regulations for Compensation for Improper Verdicts of Sedition and Communist Espionage Cases during the Martial Law Period Promulgated

The fund provides for compensating political victims and the families of those who have died. Funds (taking the form of a foundation) are to come out of the national treasury, and are not to be paid by the perpetrator of the disasters, the KMT. By October 31, 2004, a total of 5,975 cases have been granted compensation.

## July 9, 1999
### President Lee Teng-hui Proposes "Special State-to-state Relations" between Taiwan and China

Breaking free from the "one China" conundrum, the proposal defends Taiwan's international position as an autonomous entity.

## December 10, 1999
### Green Island Monument Becomes Reality

In the past, Green Island can be mentioned only in fearful whispers, but now its former horrors are given full public recognition. *See p. 52.*

## March 18, 2000
### Taiwan's First Peaceful Transfer of Power

With DPP candidate Chen Shui-bian's succesful presidential bid, the KMT's 55-year monopoly on power comes to a close.

## May 20, 2000
### President Chen Announces Human Rights Policy

In his inauguration speech, Chen Shui-bian pledges adherence to the Universal Declaration of Human Rights, incorporation of the international human rights covenants into domestic law, and the establishment of a National Human Rights Commission.

## September 28, 2001
### Army, Navy and Air Force Criminal Law Passed

Onerous punishment for military service personnel greatly reduced: the old law has 44 crimes stipulating mandatory death sentence, whereas with passage of the new law only two are capital crimes.

## August 2, 2003
### President Chen Provides Political Prisoners with Certification of Restoration of Reputation

This redressing of past wrongs is full of symbolic meaning.

## March 20, 2004
### Taiwan Conducts National Referendum

The first-ever national referendum was held, in tandem of the presidential election, in which Chen Shui-bian won his re-election. The referendum was held in response to the high tension across the Taiwan Strait, with China deploying increasing numbers of missiles targeting Taiwan. Two items were put to vote: 1) strengthen national defense capabilities; 2) cross-strait dialogue to ensure peace and stability.

## Buddhist Monks Arrested

This is a postcard mailed from Taipei to the International Committee for the Defense of Human Rights in Taiwan. To prevent interception and inspection, important information was conveyed by writing minute lettering in the square provided for the stamp, which was covered when the stamp was applied. The secret intelligence here was: "October, in Puli, arrested were Master Shao Ying, Master Shao Lung, abbot of Puli's Chiu Ling Temple."

As for repression of the clergy, all religions regard it as highly criminal. Many religious professionals were arrested during the period of Martial Law, and some were even sentenced, with at least one of them executed. Religious organizations incurring the displeasure of the authorities were infiltrated and discord was instigated among them. They were monitored, had their phones tapped (like the Presbyterian Church in Taiwan), or were banned altogether (as with I Kuan Tao and Nichiren). Religious freedom is a benchmark of human rights, but in martial-law Taiwan, the neurotic KMT regime could allow no religious leader to stand alongside the deified Chiang Kai-shek.

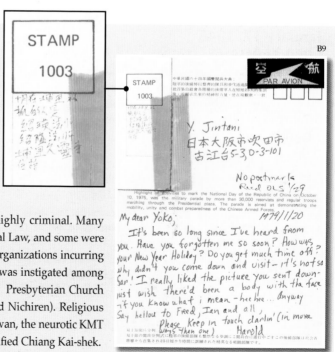

## Comrades in Confinement

This painting is richly symbolic, but also a little untrue, for at the time the prison cells were like tins of sardines, like chicken coops, like factory farms. The mass arrests of the 1950s brought in more prisoners than there was space to keep them.

Painted by Auyang Wen

# Island of Injustice
## Taiwan's Major Political Cases

In those days, Taiwan's human rights had descended into the deep.
Political cases had spread across the island like a pestilence.
"For the nation—all were commies, everyone a spy," another way
to describe the rampancy of trumped-up cases, frame-ups and fake cases.
This chapter lays out several major, representative cases in general terms.
Naturally, they are but the tip of the iceberg.

## Taipei City

### The Taipei Work Committee Case

Established in 1947, the Taipei Work Committee was headed by Kuo Hsiu-tsung, a doctor at National Taiwan University Hospital, and came under the Chinese Communists' Taiwan Provincial Work Committee (TPWC) *(see note 1)*, which had eleven chapters. After the February 28 Incident of 1947, it constituted one of the centers of the left-wing movement. Suspects caught up in January 1950 were mainly the most prominent intellectuals, including Dr. Hsu Chiang, whom the Japanese had hoped would become "Asia's first Nobel laureate." He and fourteen others were executed.

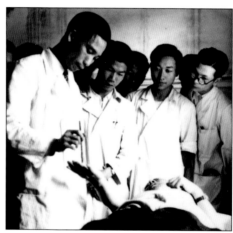

D1

Dr. Hsu Chiang, *left*, teaching clinical medicine.

### Student Work Committee Case

Student movement center for the Taiwan Provincial Work Committee, this was the biggest student movement case of the 1950s. Mainly students and young teachers, 45 suspects were taken in, with an average age of 23.7. Eleven were executed.

### Su Yi-lin Case

In 1948 high-ranking Chinese Communist cadre Yu Fei was dispatched to Taiwan to set up a complex organization among the mainlanders exiled in Taiwan. Its main purpose was to collect intelligence and to convert the resident-in-Taiwan mainlanders to the left. This was one of many such cases connected with this organization. In all, nineteen people were executed, most of them mainlanders.

### National Youth Solidarity Promotion Association Case

In the 1964 election for mayor of Taipei City, Kao Yu-shu (Henry Kao, an independent candidate) defeated the Kuomintang (KMT) candidate. Establishing the National Youth Solidarity Promotion Association after the election, students and young people who had worked in Kao's campaign linked up with Taiwan Independence organizations abroad, thereby uniting domestic and overseas forces to resist the KMT. They issued a statement, "For the Establishment of a Republic of Taiwan," but were thwarted when an undercover spy reported them. 274 were arrested, with fifteen of them getting from two to fifteen years. The Association was the first large congregation of the new Tangwai (non-KMT) generation, and was the largest case in the late sixties.

## Taipei County

### Luku Base Case

Situated in Taipei County, Luku is a poor mountain village on the edge of Taipei City. Since the Japanese period, it had served as a place of refuge for fleeing leftists. Saying that they had broken a "military base" (note 2), over ten thousand KMT troops surrounded them. 242 people were captured or turned themselves in. 36 were executed and 97 were sentenced to a combined total of 871 years. Most of the victims were simple and innocent farmers and miners. After savagely torturing and charging them with crimes, those handling the cases claimed high-dollar rewards for cracking the case.

## Keelung City

### Keelung Work Committee Case

44 people were arrested in one of the biggest cases in the early part of the White Terror period. Seven were executed, including Chung Hao-tung, principal of Keelung Middle School. Through the breaking of this case, the authorities followed leads to Tsai Hsiao-chien and other leaders of the TPWC, who in turn divulged intelligence on the whole of TPWC. Thanks to the betrayal of the leadership, the organization collapsed like a house of cards.

Li Tsang-chiang, a leader of the Keelung Work Committee, shot on October 14, 1950.

## Hsinchu County

### Chutung Cement Factory Case

This was a typical 1950s case, with young Hakka people as victims (note 3). 27-year-old Cheng Hsiang-ting, a worker at the Chutung Cement Factory, had been developing a factory-based labor movement that became a branch of the TPWC. In May 1951 he was sold out by one of his higher-ups, resulting in the execution of eight people.

## Miaoli County

### Tseng Wen-chang Case

Yet another typical political case involving the Hakka people. The TPWC had developed an organization in the simple rustic mountain areas of Miaoli, with plans to destroy a steel bridge, which they hoped would be carried out in concert with the anticipated Chinese Communist attack on Taiwan. The case was broken in March 1950, with 42 people arrested. Three were executed, with twenty people given prison terms of thirteen years. The majority of those involved were innocent farmers.

## Taoyuan County

### Chungli Incident

When, on the day of the election for county magistrate in November 1977, Chungli discovered suspected KMT vote rigging, a crowd of over ten thousand surrounded the police station. When the crowd became unruly, the police opened fire, killing two young people. For the Martial Law period, this ranked as a massive demonstration. It opened the curtain on the democratic movement, which advanced by the simultaneous use of both electoral campaigns and mass demonstrations.

The Chungli Incident

## Taichung County

### Taichung Work Committee Case

In February 1949 the TPWC established its Taichung Work Committee, organized into twelve branches, with which they were developing the left-wing movement in the Taichung area. They were busted in March 1950, with 63 people arrested. Seven were executed and twelve given life imprisonment, with the remainder sentenced to an aggregate prison term of one thousand years. Eight of them served thirty years or more, and only won release through domestic and overseas pressure.

Kuo Wan-fu, shot on September 5, 1953.

### Tachia Case

In this, the biggest of the Taiwan Democratic Self-Government League series of cases, elementary school principal Kuo Wan-fu was developing an organization in the town of Tachia and propagating anti-government literature. He was apprehended in May 1951. One hundred people were implicated. Eighteen were executed, and fourteen were sentenced to five to fifteen years.

## Changhua County

### Chen Hun-lun Case

At the time of the February 28 Incident of 1947, Chen Tsuan-ti had been leading the Yunlin People's Militia, after which he escaped to the mountains for five years. Someone ratted on him in June 1952, and he was found out.

The officials implicated others, and five people, including his nephew Chen Hun-lun, were executed, and eleven sentenced to ten years. This was the biggest case of political arrests in Changhua.

## Yunlin County

### Liao Wen-yi Taiwan Independence Case

This was actually two Taiwan Independence cases combined. In the first, May 1950 case, 119 people were arrested in the midst of the White Terror, while in the other case two hundred people were arrested, in January 1962. All of them were related to Liao Wen-yi, who was promoting Taiwan Independence from exile in Hong Kong and Japan. In 1965, the KMT authorities sentenced one of Liao's family members to death, forcing him to return to Taiwan and surrender, whereupon the Taiwan Independence movement's center of gravity shifted to the United States.

### Su Tung-chi Case

Together with some Taiwan Independence advocates, Yunlin County Councilor Su Tung-chi teamed up with a group of marines to plan an armed uprising in Yunlin. The case was broken in September 1961, with 300 people arrested. 46 were sentenced, three of them (Su Tung-chi included) to death, but active support from within and without Taiwan forced a reduction to life imprisonment. Three of the soldiers receiving heavy sentences in the case were involved in the resistance fight and breakout at Taiyuan Prison in 1970. They were caught and executed.

Liao Wen-yi (1910-1976), with background showing the flag of the Taiwan Republic. He was declared president of the republic's temporary government.

### Hung Lin-er Case

This, the largest case of political imprisonment in the county, mostly involved farmers. One of them, Hung Lin-er, was accused of counter-propaganda against the land reform's tenant rent reduction plan *(note 4)*. He was arrested in June 1950. Six were executed, 23 given five to twelve years. At the time, the KMT was implementing its stringent land reform with iron fist, and the Hung Lin-er Case served the function of falling victim to the "kill the chicken to scare the monkey" tactic.

D6

Tang Shou-jen, *left*, and Kao Yi-sheng, *right*

### Tang Shou-jen Case

County Councilor Tang Shou-jen (Tsou tribe), township mayor Kao Yi-sheng (Tsou tribe), and Taiwan Provincial Assemblyman Leshin Wadan (Atayal tribe) were promoting an Indigenous self-rule movement when they were arrested in October 1950. Including them, six people were sentenced to death. This case was representative of the KMT regime's repression of young Indigenous talent. Arrest actions continued for another twenty years, during which time many Indigenous young people and intellectuals were imprisoned.

### Li Wu-chang Case

In June 1948 the Chinese communists held a meeting in Hong Kong to discuss work in Taiwan. Those attending from Taiwan included Tsai Hsiao-chien, Kuo Hsiu-tsung and Li Wu-chang. Upon returning to Taiwan, Li set up an organization in Tainan, but it was broken up when Tsai Hsiao-chien provided a list of those who had attended the Hong Kong meeting. Forty were arrested, sixteen sentenced to death.

### Tainan Work Committee Case

The resistance movement in Tainan, the old-time cultural capital of Taiwan, has a long tradition. In 1947 it had already seen the establishment of the Tainan Work Committee, which, coming under the TPWC, was advancing the left-wing movement. It was broken up in 1950, with most of those implicated being teachers and students. Ten were executed, 22 given sentences ranging from five to fifteen years.

### Matou Case

In this, the first case of wrongful imprisonment in the history of Taiwan elections, in 1950 Matou Township mayor Hsieh Jui-jen defeated the pro-KMT candidate, thereby winning a second term. The authorities made a big case out of it, and Hsieh and two others were sentenced to death, nine to life, and fourteen to terms of ten to fifteen years. Four people, including Lin Su-yang and Li Chin-mu, spent 34 years in prison, which set the record for time served behind bars.

## Kaohsiung County

### Shih Ming-teh Taiwan Independence Case

Following on the Su Tung-chi case of 1961, this was another big Taiwan Independence case. A number of army men (including Shih Ming-teh) and university students set up the Taiwan Independence League, but were later reported by an undercover spy. Arrests came in May 1962, with 24 people receiving heavy sentences.

### Kaohsiung Incident

Coming on International Human Rights Day in 1979, this was the largest-scale repression of dissidents after the mass arrests of the 1950s. According to official figures, over one hundred people were arrested, with nearly all of Tangwai's best and brightest taken in. Eight of them were tried in military court and sentenced to terms ranging from twelve years to life, while 33 were tried in civil court. Another ten were sentenced to terms for harboring fugitive Shih Ming-teh. When the defendants appeared in court and revealed the tortures they had suffered, this brought the cruel methods used on political prisoners before international scrutiny.

## Pingtung County

### Wu Nai-kuang Case

In December 1951, four teachers who had come to Taiwan from the mainland, including the painter Huang Jung-tsan, were arrested, accused of using educational culture work as a cover to promote rebellion, and executed.

## Ilan County

### Chunghsing Paper Factory Case

After being established by the Japanese, the largest paper factory in Southeast Asia was taken over by the KMT. Having joined the Taiwan Democratic Self-Government League, in 1952 some of the workers at the factory were accused by the authorities of fomenting rebellion. Twenty were arrested, seven sentenced to death.

## Taitung County

### Taiyuan Prison Breakout

With the demolition of the Green Island New Life Correction Center in 1965, the political prisoners being held there were transferred to Taiyuan Prison in Taitung. In February 1970 some of them planned to seize a radio station to broadcast news of Taiwan's rule of terror to the world. Six of them escaped and were later caught. Five of them were executed.

Chan Tien-tseng, *second from the left,* and Chen Liang, *first on the right,* both of whom were executed as leaders in the Taiyuan Prison Breakout Incident, shown here with their comrades, in 1969.

## Penghu Islands

### Penghu Case

Some 8000 teachers and students from Shantung on the mainland fled to Taiwan in July 1949, stopping for a time at Penghu en route. There the military tried to forcibly make conscripts of the students, whereupon two school principals stood up to protect them. Together with five of the students, they were executed. One hundred students were sent to prison, and thousands were forced into the military.

## Armed Forces

### Sun Li-jen Case

A graduate of Virginia Military Academy in the United States, Sun Li-jen was a high-ranking Chinese officer, having once served as commander-in-chief of the army. With his American background, he opposed having the military under party control, an arrangement which Chiang Ching-kuo had learned in the Soviet Union. In June 1955, on the pretext that someone serving under him was a communist spy, Sun Li-jen was stripped of his military rights and put under house arrest for 33 years. 300 military officers were implicated. The "Butcher of Kaohsiung," Peng Meng-chi swiftly moved up the ranks to take Sun's place.

## Police Forces

### Cheng Chen-yen Case

When the KMT came to Taiwan after the war, they consolidated their absolute rule by flooding Taiwan with police and secret police. There were sometimes struggles between the two, this case being an example. Cheng Chen-yen was arrested in February 1950 upon accusations that there was a rebel organization afoot among police circles. He and five others were executed. In another case two months later, the chiefs of the Hsinchu City and Taichung County police departments were arrested and executed together with the other three.

## Education

### Hsiung Yen-kuang Case

In June 1953, on the pretext that educational circles had been infiltrated by "communist spies," school principals, teachers and normal-education students were arrested throughout the island. They were of the highest caliber, and were even able to produce official documentation in their

Hsiung Yen-kuang, shot on November 8, 1955.

favor, but they were seen as "masters of disguise," and in the end six were executed, one given fifteen years, and the rest sentenced to reform camp.

## Academia

### National Taiwan University Department of Philosophy Case

"Professional students" covered the campuses in Taiwan of martial law days. With universities headed by important KMT figures, and academic freedom but a dream, from December 1972 to June 1975, eight professors in the NTU philosophy department were falsely accused and convicted in a case perpetrated by the KMT, the military and the "professional students." The school would not continue their contracts. Many other teachers met with similar treatment in mainly individual cases.

## The Media

### Lei Chen Free China Case

In martial law times, the media in Taiwan had two choices: either play the mouthpiece of the KMT, or get eradicated. A typical case of the sixties was that of Lei Chen's *Free China Fortnightly*, while at the *Public Forum* (1947~1967, newspaper founded by democratic leader Li Wan-chu), a bunch of editors and reporters, from the chief editor on down, went to prison.

In May 1957, the intelligence authorities wanted to fabricate a case involving "communist spies infiltrating media circles to await Taiwan's liberation by the Chinese communist military forces, at which time they would take over." Five media professionals were arrested, and their head, Lin Chen-ting, was given a life sentence. In both the Huang Er-tsun Case of September 1957 and the Li Ching-sun Case of December 1970, two high-level journalists were convicted of rebellion.

Radio engineer Wang Sheng-ho, *left*, and Li Peng, *right*, former reporter for the *New York Times* and *Time* magazine. Accused of being spies working for the GPU (predecessor of the KGB), they were shot on September 6, 1950.

## Literature and Arts

### A Long List of Oppressed Artists

Having met with repugnance from the literary community while on the mainland, once the KMT had arrived in Taiwan it mercilessly adopted politically repressive measures directed at the literati and artists. A list of those caught up in one repression after another: movie producer Pai Ke (shot), playwright Chien Kuo-hsien (shot), poet Lan Ming-ku (shot), author Yang Kui (12 years), writer Po Yang (12 years), movie star Yang Wei-hsi (12 years), broadcast announcer Tsui Hsiao-ping (12 years), modern dance choreographer Tsai Jui-yueh (3 years), painter Hsieh Li-fa (blacklisted, unable to return to Taiwan)....

## Overseas

### Henry Liu Murder Case

In October 1984 the head of the Ministry of National Defense Intelligence Bureau, Wang Hsi-ling, dispatched three killers from the Bamboo Union to the US to shoot Liu Yi-liang (Henry Liu), a Chinese-American author and writer of a Chiang Ching-kuo biography and of many behind-the-curtain exposés of the KMT *(note 5)*. That the KMT should be so blatant as to murder an American within the US enraged Americans of all stripes. The KMT sentenced three to life, and in November of the same year, over a hundred Bamboo Union members were arrested and incarcerated at Green Island.

D11

Pastors with the Presbyterian Church in Taiwan: Hsu Tien-hsien, *left*, and Rev. Daniel Beeby, from the UK. For having a hand in the PCT's "Statement on Our National Fate," Beeby was kicked out of Taiwan as an "unfriendly person." This is the political repression suffered by foreigners in Taiwan.

## The Prisons

### Three Murder Cases

At least three large-scale murders of prisoners were carried out by the KMT authorities to deal with unruly political prisoners. The KMT said that these political prisoners were organizing and fomenting rebellion, so they were indicted again and executed. Five were executed in the February 1951 Martial Law Section Jail case, fourteen in the April 1953 New Life Correction Center case, and fourteen in the May 1953 Hsintien Military Prison case.

## Secret Police

### MBIS–vs–CBIS Faction Fight

Having gone through the insane spy-eradication campaigns of the fifties, two KMT secret police factions—the Military Bureau of Investigation and Statistics (MBIS) and the Central Bureau of Investigation and Statistics (CBIS) —went at each other's throats in the sixties. In order to purge the CBIS, Chiang Ching-kuo had the MBIS take over the Bureau of Investigation and accuse some of the higher CBIS officers of being spies. The latter were all experts in spy cases, but now it was their turn to play the spies *(note 6)*. They were to get a taste of the medicine that they had administered to so many others: cruel torture and trumped-up charges. In the end, some of them were sentenced to death, and at least one killed himself in prison.

# Political Assassinations

## From Exterminating Families to Political Traffic Accidents

Aside from sentencing them in court, the KMT also used assassination against the Taiwan opposition—a fascist method for which they were infamous while on the mainland. In February 1948, the head of the Chinese Literature Department at National Taiwan University, Hsu Shou-shang, was assassinated. In the 1960s, Hung Kuo-shih, a Communist Party member of long experience who had made a fresh start with the KMT, was murdered. On February 28, 1980, the mother and twin daughters of the talented young lawyer Lin Yi-hsiung were slaughtered. In July 1981, when Dr. Chen Wen-chen returned to Taiwan from the US, he was called in for questioning by the Taiwan Garrison Command and mysteriously died shortly after.

Another commonplace method of assassination was to manufacture a traffic accident with anti-government people as targets, whether as a way of scaring them or as a way of settling scores. The most-cited example is that of Wu Shu-jen, wife of the current president, Chen Shui-bian. In 1985 she was run over and seriously injured, so that even now she must use a wheelchair to get around.

## Notes

1. The Taiwan Provincial Work Committee was a Chinese Communist Party organization working underground in Taiwan. Established by Tsai Hsiao-chien in 1946, by the time of the wholesale arrests of May 1950, it had only 900-plus CCP members. The number of those shot during the White Terror was at least in the thousands, with tens of thousands unjustly sentenced—proving the ruthlessness and extreme severity with which the KMT dealt with human rights.

2. From the number of weapons discovered when the officials said that they had broken some "military base cases," it can be seen that there were no "bases" worthy of the name. In several instances they were even unable to find any bullets. As a former high-ranking officer in the Security Bureau conceded later, this was owing to the cases having to be fabricated, since Chiang Kai-shek had ordered that "all effort would go to the eradication of the military bases."

3. In simple terms, the residents of Taiwan could be divided into four main ethnic groups. In order of size: Hoklo, Mainlander, Hakka, Indigenous. The Mainlanders were those who had followed the KMT into exile in Taiwan in 1949. In principle, there was no difference between the oppression suffered by these four groups.

4. The tenant rent reduction plan, by which the landlord's share of the harvest could not exceed 37.5 percent, was the first of three steps in the Land Reform Program. High-pressure methods were used to promote it, thereby weakening the power of the people to challenge the rulers, and laying the foundation for the KMT's dictatorial rule.

5. The Bamboo Union is a Mainlander underground gang. The KMT's rise to strength and prominence was related to Mainlander gangs. In the early period, gangster elements entered the secret police. In the 1990s, the KMT tolerated entry of gangland power into politics, one of the reasons for the Taiwan's political chaos today.

6. In Taiwan, the proper meaning of "communist spy" was really "anyone the KMT didn't like." Because of the requirements of political struggle, everyone had the potential for being named a "communist spy," where in fact only a tiny minority of "communist spies" actually had anything to do with the Chinese communists. The same rationale lay behind use of "counterrevolutionary elements" and "KMT agents" to accuse dissidents and innocent people in China.

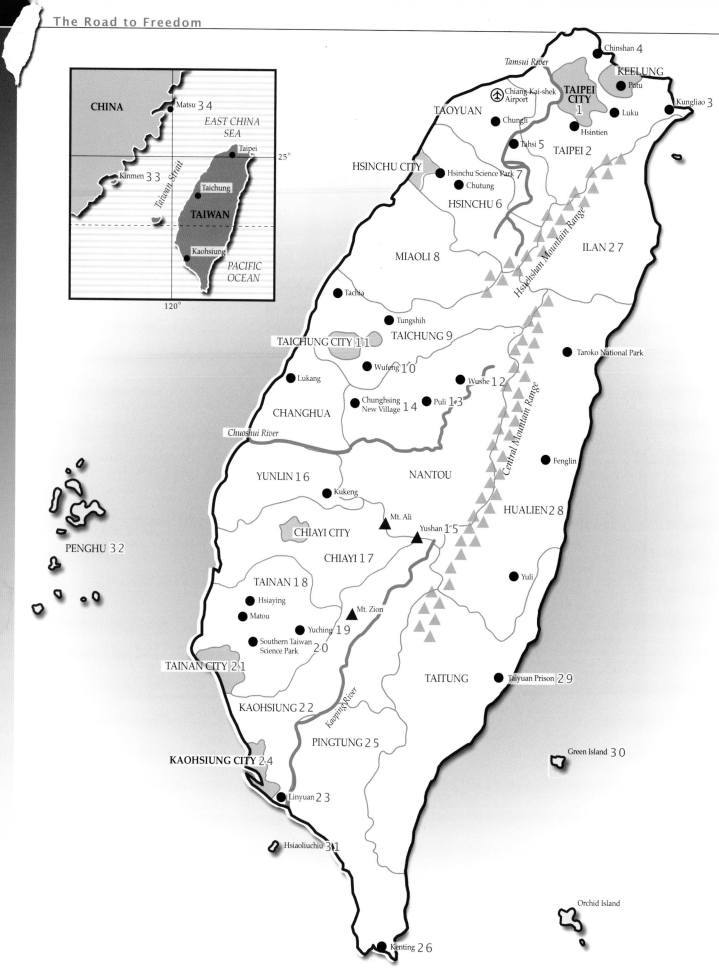

1 **TAIPEI CITY**
Capital of Taiwan, pop. 2.6 million (2004)

2 **TAIPEI**
With a population of 3.7 million (2004), Taiwan's largest county

3 **Kungliao**
Taiwan's fourth nuclear power plant, object of much controversy

4 **Chinshan**
Taiwan's first nuclear power plant

5 **Tahsi**
Home of the preserved remains of Chiang Kai-shek and his son, where many KMT officials have come to pay reverence and swear undying allegiance

6 **HSINCHU**
Hakka people hold the majority

7 **Hsinchu Science Park**
Founded in 1980, one of the world's largest infotech industrial parks, with 370 companies in operation and combined sales of 24 billion dollars in 2003

8 **MIAOLI**
Hakka people in the majority

9 **TAICHUNG**
Mid-Taiwan's flourishing metropolis

10 **Wufeng**
Site of former Taiwan Provincial Assembly, up to the 1970s center of gravity for parliamentarian politics

11 **TAICHUNG CITY**
Pop. 1 million in 2004, largest city in central Taiwan

12 **Wushe**
In 1930, over 1000 killed by Japanese in Taiwan's largest Indigenous uprising

13 **Puli⁺**
Site of Feb. 28 Incident's most heated battle, in which several dozen students overcame over 700 KMT troops

14 **Chunghsing New Village**
Seat of the former Taiwan Provincial Government

15 **Yushan**
At 3997 meters, Taiwan's tallest peak, symbol of Formosan pride

16 **YUNLIN**
Agriculture predominates in both Changhua and Yunlin

17 **CHIAYI**
Agriculture predominates

18 **TAINAN**
Agriculture predominates

19 **Yuching**
6000 killed by Japanese in Chiaopanien Massacre (1915-16)

20 **Southern Taiwan Science Park**
Taiwan's second infotech industrial park

21 **TAINAN CITY**
Old-time cultural capital and stronghold of the opposition movement

22 **KAOHSIUNG**
The center of Taiwan's industrial might, also home to both accumulated wealth and industrial pollution

23 **Linyuan**
In 1988 petrochemical plant surrounded by 20,000 people protesting water pollution

24 **KAOHSIUNG CITY**
1947 KMT-perpetrated massacre and 1979 mass arrests, together making Taiwan's second-largest city cradle of the democratic movement. Pop. 1.5 million (2004)

25 **PINGTUNG**
Taiwan's tropical county

26 **Kenting**
One of Taiwan's premier vacationing spots, next to Taiwan's third nuclear power plant

27 **ILAN**
Birthplace of traditional Taiwanese opera and important stronghold of the movement for democracy and human rights

28 **HUALIEN**
Home of the world-famous Taroko Gorge

29 **Taiyuan Prison⁎**
Constructed in 1962 using confiscated prisoner property, it held several hundred political prisoners

30 **Green Island⁎**
For over 30 years served as Taiwan's largest political prison—over 1600 at its peak

31 **Hsiaoliuchiu⁎**
Gangsters imprisoned here, but in early 1960s KMT authorities originally planned to build special prison here holding 3000, but switched to Taiyuan prison for lack of funds

32 **PENGHU**
With 64 small islands, first Taiwan area to know development (in the 12th century)

33 **Kinmen**
4000 killed and injured between August and October 1958, with PRC expending nearly half a million shells in the worst crisis of the Taiwan Strait

34 **Matsu**
Along with Kinmen, closest ROC territory to the PRC, serving as military bases in the cold war, but Kinmen now a transit point for passage between the two sides

⁺ Places mentioned in the text and figuring in the February 28 Incident
⁎ Places mentioned in the text and figuring in the White Terror

# Under the Gloomy Sky
## Prison and Execution Ground Maps

**From prison purgatory to the execution grounds, in this,
the bleakest and dreariest of times in the annals of Taiwan human rights,
people's lives were no different from those of beasts.**

### ■ Taipei: White Terror Main Camp

During Martial Law, Taipei was Taiwan's spy factory and wholesale center for political prisoners. At least tens of thousands of political dissidents and innocents were all brought here for indictment and, once labeled rebels, were sent hither and yon to serve their sentences.

### ■ Political Repression Trilogy: Investigation, Sentencing and Imprisonment or Execution

#### Step one: interrogation

The secret police and their organizations, from central to local levels, could arrest at will and exact a confession using all kinds of torture. For the political prisoners, it was this step that was the greatest ordeal, both physically and mentally.

- - - - - - - - - - - - - - - - - - - - - - - - - - - - - - - - - - - - -

#### Step two: sentencing

Mainly the Martial Law Section (for military law sentencing), and second to that the courts (civil code sentencing of opponents), were both dispensing "justice" according to directions coming from the KMT.

- - - - - - - - - - - - - - - - - - - - - - - - - - - - - - - - - - - - -

#### Step three: imprisonment or execution

Those sentenced to imprisonment were sent to the concentration camp on Green Island for labor reform, while for thought reform they were sent to the Tucheng Production Education Experiment Center or just incarcerated at the Hsintien Military Prison or at Taiyuan Prison. Those condemned to death were shot on the banks of the Hsintien River at either Babacho (the Racetrack) or the Ankeng Execution Grounds.

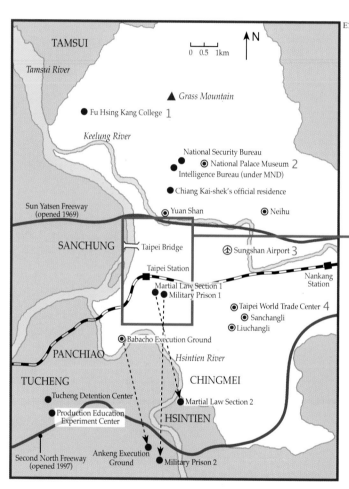

1 Created by Chiang Ching-kuo in 1951, it trained cadres who played the part of thought police. Their duties, assigned by the party, were to play "political officer" in the military and schools.

2 One of the largest museums in the world, it is the repository for a huge collection of age-old Chinese pieces. The Taiwan authorities have used it to make the claim that Taiwan is the preserver of Chinese traditional culture.

3 Until the opening of the Chiang Kai-shek Airport in Taoyuan, this was Taiwan's only international airport.

4 Built in 1986, it now hosts the second largest annual information technology show in the world. The nearby Taipei 101 Building was completed in 2004, becoming, at 508 meters, the tallest building in the world. In the 1950s, this was all desolate, undeveloped land.

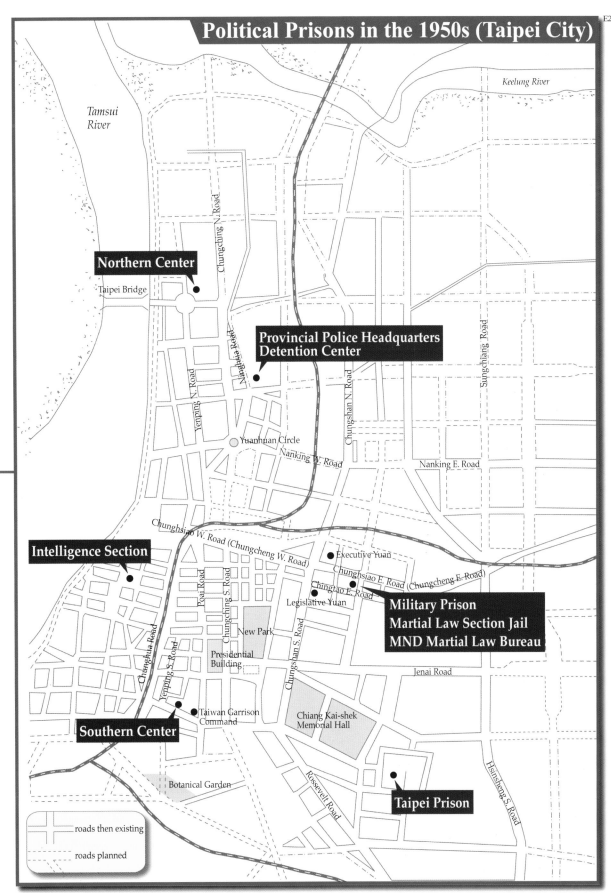

# Political Prisons in the 1950s (Taipei City)

E2

*Tamsui River*

*Keelung River*

**Northern Center**

Taipei Bridge

Chungching N. Road

**Provincial Police Headquarters Detention Center**

Ninghsia Road

Yenping N. Road

Chungshan N. Road

Sungchiang Road

Yuanhuan Circle

Nanking W. Road

Nanking E. Road

Chunghsiao W. Road (Chungcheng W. Road)

**Intelligence Section**

Poai Road

Chungching S. Road

Chunghua Road

• Executive Yuan

Chunghsiao E. Road (Chungcheng E. Road)

Chingtao E. Road

Legislative Yuan

**Military Prison
Martial Law Section Jail
MND Martial Law Bureau**

Chungshan S. Road

New Park

Presidential Building

Yenping S. Road

Jenai Road

• Taiwan Garrison Command

Chiang Kai-shek Memorial Hall

**Southern Center**

Botanical Garden

Roosevelt Road

Hsinsheng S. Road

• **Taipei Prison**

roads then existing

roads planned

By Chen Meng-ho, based on 1949 Taipei City map

## Chicken Cages and Pig Sties: Locking Up the Prisoners of Conscience

Prior to sentencing, all political prisoners were locked up in the prisons of the secret police organs. According to the oral histories provided by the victims, the inhuman treatment perpetrated by these prisons included:

- overcrowded cells: one had to sleep squatting or standing.
- serious lack of exercise: resulting in constipation, hemorrhoids and other maladies.
- stinking cells: stench of sweat, urine and excrement was overwhelming all day long.
- poor air circulation: unbearably hot summers, cold and dark in winter, no hot water for bathing.
- lighting ghostly dark: no sky to be seen, pale-skinned prisoners, weakened constitutions.

- rotted-out flooring: seeping water; sleeping in such conditions invited arthritis.
- vermin and filth: cockroaches rampant, mosquitoes, bugs, lice, fleas, strange never-ending itches.
- severe nutritional insufficiency: no fish, no meat, even vegetables were short, barely enough to stave off starvation.

Once sentenced and sent off to their respective prisons, the political prisoners were treated somewhat better. But much inhuman management persisted. This was especially true of the prison at Green Island, where they had everything from the pillbox to midnight beatings *(see note 1)*. All these show the horrors of concentration camp treatment.

# Detention: Interrogation

*Units belonging to the secret police system*

### Intelligence Section*

**Location:** Hsimenting, Taipei's busiest area. It came under the Taiwan Security Command *(note 2)*.

**History:** A temple during the Japanese occupation, the KMT government converted it to a prison. Infamous for cruelty. In the late 1940s and early 1950s, many political prisoners were taken from here and secretly shot.

**Cells:** Wood construction, with twenty people to a cell totaling 10 m$^2$ (110 ft$^2$), one slept standing up; there were also coffin-like solitary confinement cells (80cm by 2 meters).

**Sub-station:** Liuchangli (SE corner of Taipei), where some cases were investigated in a mountain cave; those dying of torture would be buried in the cemetery over the mountains.

E3

Intelligence Section

### Southern Center*

**Location:** Yenping South Road, near the Presidential Building; came under the Ministry of National Defense's Security Bureau *(note 3)*.

**History:** Famed for its cruelty, it was the officers' brig of the Taiwan Military Command (Japan's highest intelligence branch in Taiwan) during the Japanese occupation, while

after the war the Taiwan Military Command location was taken over by the Defense Ministry's Security Bureau, and the prison was used to hold political prisoners.

**Cells:** Completely enclosed, with foul air, lice and mosquitoes rampant, thirty or more people confined to 30 m$^2$ (320 ft$^2$).

### Northern Center*

**Location:** Yenping North Road, near Taipei Bridge (connecting Taipei and Sanchung); came under the Ministry of National Defense's Security Bureau.

**History:** What with the Southern Center's considerable overcrowding owing to the increasing number of political prisoners, this privately-owned machinery fabricating plant

was drafted into service.

**Cells:** Of wood construction; rats had free run; oppressively damp, so dark one didn't know night from day, but not so crowded as the Southern Center, so one could sleep lying down. Meals were the worst, consisting of nothing more than thin broth with a few scraps of radish in it.

## Sanchangli Detention Center*

**Location:** Wuhsing Street, near today's Taipei World Trade Center, came under the Bureau of Investigation *(note 4)*, and was the most-dreaded of that agency's secret prisons.

**Cells:** Eerily dark and cramped; absolute seclusion; interrogation room lined with sound dampeners; famous for savagery that could even prove fatal.

**Prisoners' treatment:** Water intake limited to 500cc daily, no talking allowed, nor coughing, nor wearing of glasses, nor eating of a second bowl of rice; to prevent suicide, no pants fasteners, so one had to hold one's pants up while walking.

## Provincial Police Headquarters Detention Center

**Location:** Ninghsia Road, a 1930s-era wood structure. It came under the Taiwan Provincial Police.

**Prisoners' treatment:** Water for brushing teeth and for washing had to be gotten from the squat toilet. Of its torture methods, the most famous was the "water cell."

**Agencies:** During the White Terror many agencies were arresting. In addition to the secret services, the Army, Navy, Air Force, Joint Logistics Command, Military Police, Provincial Police Headquarters, and various local police forces could all arrest, interrogate and torture.

# Detention: Sentencing

## Martial Law Section Jail

Coming under the Taiwan Security Command (or its successor, the Taiwan Garrison Command), the Martial Law Section tried all cases of "rebellion." Here prisoners awaited sentencing by the military tribunal in insufferably crowded conditions. Once the verdicts were rendered, those getting the death sentence were immediately taken to the execution grounds and shot, while the rest were moved to the nearby military stockade *(note 5)*, and then transferred to Green Island or elsewhere to serve out their sentences.

**Location:** Chingtao East Road, near the Executive Yuan and Legislative Yuan. In 1968 the jail was moved to Hsintien, and part of the original building was rebuilt as today's five-star Lai Lai Sheraton Hotel.

**History:** Army warehouse during the Japanese occupation.

**Cells:** Wooden structure, 30 people to a 20-square-meter cell, with no room for movement. Thick with bedbugs and lice, their flooring was damp the year round with an unbearable stench. So great was the pressure that women stopped menstruating.

**Sub-station:** In Hsintien, next door to the Hsintien Military Prison *(note 6)*.

The present-day Sheraton Hotel in Taipei used to be the site of an important political prison.

Surrounded by high walls and barbed wire are the Martial Law Section of the Taiwan Security Command (left) and the Martial Law Bureau of the Ministry of National Defense (with the roof showing on the right). The Martial Law Bureau was the behind-the-scenes organization controlling sentencing of political prisoners.

# Detention: Serving Time

## Production Education Experiment Center

Located in Tucheng, Taipei County, the center belonged to the Taiwan Garrison Command. Its regimen consisted mainly of thought reform (reading, classes and meetings), and secondarily labor reform. Prisoners with one or two years left to serve were sent here for brainwashing. They had neither freedom of expression nor freedom of silence. If their views did not accord with expectations of the prison authorities, they would not be released upon completion of sentence.

## Green Island New Life Correction Center and Oasis Villa

Located on a solitary island off Taiwan's southeast coast, the Green Island New Life Correction Center (1951~65) was a labor reform concentration camp, while the Oasis Villa (1972~87, also known as the Green Island Correction Prison) was completely enclosed. *See p. 52.*

## Tucheng Detention Center

Built in 1975 in Tucheng, Taipei County, it came under the Taipei District Court. In the latter part of the White Terror period, when the KMT regime used civil law to persecute the democratic movement, those convicted served their sentences here. The current president, Chen Shui-bian, and former founder of *Freedom Era* magazine, Cheng Nan-jung, were among those who served their sentences here.

## Ministry of National Defense Military Prison

Originally on Chingtao East Road next to the Martial Law Section, overcrowding later forced it to relocate to Ankeng in Hsintien. From then on, up until 1961, the Hsintien Military Prison and the Green Island New Life Correction Center were the two most important political prisons. Later Hsintien became primarily a detention center for military offenders, with fewer political prisoners—mainly those with relatively long sentences or those of a rather special character, like Lei Chen, Su Tung-chi and Huang Hsin-chieh.

The military prison was completely sealed off, and was used exclusively for incarcerating people under the strictest, military-style management. Since military inmates and political offenders were locked up

E6

Hsintien Military Prison

in the same cell together, the military were often used to beat or rat on the political offenders, even to the point of manufacturing a bogus incident in 1953, in which fourteen political prisoners lost their lives.

## Taipei Station: Death Notice Bulletin Board

Political prisoners who were shot had their names posted on a bulletin board outside Taipei Station. At first their names were also published in the newspaper, but then the number of executions and the guilty consciences of officialdom combined to end public announcement of executions.

## Taiyuan Prison

Located in Tungho Township, Taitung County, it was built in 1962. Completely enclosed, it had two concrete cellblocks. In the summer it was insufferably hot and suffocating. Those not serving life sentences were allowed to go outside on work details, some of them going into the mountains for logging. After the prison breakout of 1970, the relatively lax administration gave way to extremely tight control. Some of those suspected of having participated in the breakout had their sentences extended by anywhere from a few months to three years.

Taiyuan was hidden deep in a mountain valley. Shown here is Kuo Chen-chun, one of the rare Taiwan independence case prisoners of the 1950s. He did 22 years in prison.

# Execution Grounds

## The Racetrack (Babacho)

**Location:** On the banks of the Hsintien River on the southwest edge of Taipei, near the Youth Park. There is now a Racetrack Memorial Park there.

**History:** During the Japanese period, it was a racetrack, hence the name.

**The grounds:** No fixed spot; anywhere along the expanse of the riverbank was a killing ground. The MPs would leave once the executions were carried out, leaving the bodies to be collected by funeral parlors.

**Comparison:** From 1927 to 1949, when China was under Kuomintang control, the vast majority of 100,000 people executed at Yuhuatai in Nanjing were political prisoners and innocents. Yuhuatai was next to the river to the south of Nanjing, just as Babacho was on the riverbank to the south of Taipei.

Racetrack Memorial Park

## Ankeng

Located near the banks of the Hsintien River, it was next door to the Hsintien Military Prison in Taipei County. From the mid-1950s onward, it replaced Babacho as the political prisoner execution ground. Construction was overseen by Pao Chi-huang, head of the MND Martial Law Bureau.

Because of his own many foul deeds, he too was executed here. In the late 1980s, the construction of the Second North Freeway uncovered a lot of corpses (over 4000, it is said) still cuffed and shackled, the trademark treatment for prisoners *(note 7)*.

## Other Locations

In 1949 or thereabouts, many refugees who accompanied the Kuomintang government in its flight from mainland China were killed without trial. Many were shot on boats and immediately dumped in the ocean, while others were captured by the secret police in Taiwan, taken to a central location and butchered en masse (one such place that has been identified is near the Wanfang MRT Station in southeast Taipei, site of an abandoned coal mine). Since they were mainlanders, they had neither relatives nor fixed domicile in Taiwan, so, since the officials have likely obliterated the evidence, it is difficult to estimate just how many died in this way.

## Disposition of the Bodies

1. Once the funeral parlor had retrieved the body and contacted the family of the deceased, they would demand a very sizeable ransom (the equivalent of a public official's five months' salary).
2. If the ransom was more than the family could afford, or if it were the body of a solitary mainlander who had come over without a family, then it would be handed directly over to the military for use in their hospital's dissection room, or else would be interred in the burial mound at Liuchangli, or buried at what is now the Second North Freeway or some such place. There the bones have lain for decades, with no one to tend them, to honor them or to remember. These were regarded as the most tragic of destinies for the deceased.
3. As for the bones buried elsewhere, they still await another time to see the light of day.

E9

Gravestones of those who met their end during the White Terror were turned up in Liuchangli. The grave, *foreground*, of Mainlander seaman Lin An-chia. He and five co-defendants were executed in 1951.

## Notes

1. *Situated at the side of the sea, the pillbox was low and cramped, with room enough to crouch but not to stand up. Baked in the hot sun by day, it was cold at night. Meals consisted of a bowl of rice and salt water, and no more. If one came out of it alive after ten days, it was all one could do to breathe. In the eyes of the authorities, no sooner was a political prisoner brought to the New Life Correction Center than he fell to plotting rebellion, so often inmates were called out of their beds in the middle of the night, and hauled off to Eel Ditch along the wall of the center for torture and interrogation.*

2. *Established in 1949, the Taiwan Security Command's first commander was Peng Meng-chi, the "Butcher of Kaohsiung" in the February 28 Incident. Besides executing prisoners in secret, the TSC had a Martial Law Section so as to cover the sentencing of everyone accused of rebellion with legalistic packaging. In 1958 it was made over as the Taiwan Garrison Command, Taiwan's version of the KGB.*

3. *Established in 1946, the Security Bureau was a descendant of the Military Bureau of Investigation and Statistics (MBIS), one of the Kuomintang government's two big secret police systems (the other being the Central Bureau of Investigation and Statistics, CBIS). The MBIS undertook assassinations and kidnappings of political dissidents, and their incarceration in fascist concentration camps. It also carried out a massacre of political prisoners in Chongqing in November 1949. In the Taiwan of the 1950s, it was mainly the Security Bureau that handled the important political cases. In 1955 it was reorganized as the Ministry of National Defense Intelligence Bureau.*

4. *The Ministry of Justice Bureau of Investigation (BOI), whose forerunner was the CBIS (est. 1938), was the civilian branch of the secret police and had offices throughout Taiwan. Since the 1960s it was one of the two main forces for suppression of human rights, the other one being the Taiwan Garrison Command, which was the military branch.*

5. *Located near the military prison, the Martial Law Section utilized the massive labor force of its inmates, taking government contracts on such jobs as quarrying sand and gravel from the riverbed, doing laundry, sewing apparel, and finishing decorations. Although the work was onerous, it went virtually unpaid (a day's labor might earn one enough to pay for a couple of bus fares), but it allowed for greater freedom of movement, so many applied. Thus, many of Taipei's early-period structures owe their existence to these unsung heroes.*

6. *In his prison memoirs,* Talking About the Martial Law Section Jail in Chingmei — *mistitled because the jail was actually in Hsintien — veteran human rights activist Hsieh Tsung-min reveals that the mountains around Chingmei were home to a secret prison housing political prisoners, and that, of all those who were sent there, not one returned. The many cruel tortures there included medical experiments.*

7. *Before a political prisoner was executed, handcuffs and shackles weighing from three to five kilograms were applied. Shackles were also used as punishment for those who resisted prison authority.*

Green Island During the White Terror I

# New Life Correction Center (1951~1965)

## Camp Scenes

F1

**Elephant's Nose Rock**
Named for its shape.

Elephant's Nose Rock

New Camp Area

Sports Area

Command Station

Administrative Center

### Layout
The concentration camp was divided into three battalions, each with four squadrons housed in a long barracks.
Painter: Chen Meng-ho (1930~ ), Taipei City. Arrested in 1952 because of a false charge brought against him by a "professional student" classmate, and sentenced to fifteen years.

F2

**Human Rights Monument**
Inaugurated on December 10, 1999. In the background are Tri-Peak Rock and General's Rock.

## Bird's Eye Side View
Painted in 1998.

F3

F4

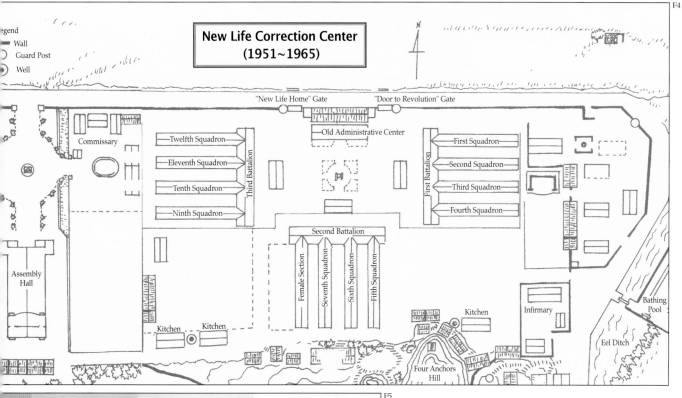

### New Life Correction Center (1951~1965)

Legend
- Wall
- Guard Post
- Well

"New Life Home" Gate    "Door to Revolution" Gate

Commissary

Twelfth Squadron
Eleventh Squadron
Tenth Squadron
Ninth Squadron
Third Battalion

Old Administrative Center

First Squadron
Second Squadron
Third Squadron
Fourth Squadron
First Battalion

Second Battalion
Female Section
Seventh Squadron
Sixth Squadron
Fifth Squadron

Assembly Hall

Kitchen    Kitchen

Kitchen

Infirmary

Bathing Pool

Eel Ditch

Four Anchors Hill

F5

## The Camp and the Villa
The wide, open space facing the sea is now for the Green Island Human Rights Memorial Park. Its range is for the most part the same as the New Life Correction Center. Most of the center buildings are in ruins, while others have been cleared away, though some have been converted to a Skills Training Center (the red-roofed structures on the right). Oasis Villa buildings (lower left) have, on the other hand, mostly preserved their original appearance.

## The Great Wall

Seen in the distance is the wall of the camp, nicknamed the "Great Wall" by political prisoner wits. It was built by the prisoners themselves with reef rocks.

## Kenan ("Roughing It") Buildings

The camp's barracks in which the prisoners and staff lived were all wooden, but there were once a number of sheds built from reef rocks. They had thatched roofs and were used for storage or activities. Only one remains.

F9

## Bird's Eye Frontal View
Painted in 2002

F10

## Tri-Peak Rock and General's Rock
The most obvious landmarks in the area around the camp.

## Great Wall Site
Now only a short section of around sixty meters remains. Two political prisoners, Auyang Wen, *left*, and Chen Meng-ho, *right*, excelled in painting and photography. They were the only officially designated photographers in the camp.

F11

F12

## Pillbox

Used both for prisoner confinement and as a shore defense sentry post, this seaside pillbox was located beside General's Rock.

## Swallow Cave

A natural cave, *below and right*, at the cape near the camp. Cool inside, it was like an arched auditorium. The prisoners built a stage out of reef rocks deep inside the cave (the platform where the men are standing), as a place to rehearse entertainment activities.

F13

F14

## Public Grave

Anyone who died in an accident or though suicide, injury, or sickness but who had no one to collect his remains was buried here. There were twelve squadrons in the camp, and this one was called the Thirteenth Squadron.

F15

F16

## Green Island Park
Originally located on the slope behind the camp, later submerged when a dam was built on the upper reach of Eel Ditch.

F17

## Upper Reach of Eel Ditch
This is the only fresh water source in long-term use at the camp.

# Political Prisoner Activities

F18

### Vegetable Garden

Green Island is subject to strong and salty wind from the ocean and was originally quite sparse in vegetation. Many political prisoners with farming experience or a background in agricultural science overcame various difficulties to plant a large and impressive garden, notable for the quality and quantity of its produce. It was a "green miracle."

F19

### Grazing Cows

Put out to graze on the grassy slopes around the prison, the cows as well as their prisoner tenders were both kept under close observation.

F20

### Raising Livestock

The camp had to be self-supplying in terms of food, so the political prisoners raised pigs, cows, and chickens to improve their diet.

F21

## Political Education Classes

The curriculum included Sun Yat-sen's *Three Principles of the People*, as well as KMT anti-communist dogma, such as *History of Russo-Soviet Aggression, Communist Bandit Brutality, Chiang Kai-shek in Word and Deed, Criticizing Maoism*. After class the prisoners had to engage in discussion and write about how they had profited.

## Shopping Coupons

Limited to use in the camp. The money sent to prisoners by family members could be exchanged for coupons at a 1:1 ratio. This prevented private transactions with the local populace and served as a rich financial resource for the camp.

F23                    F24

## Swearing Oaths

Political prisoners were repeatedly compelled to shout KMT slogans and swear oaths of loyalty to the KMT regime.

F22

F25

F26

## Female Section

There were almost one hundred women in the camp. To keep them separate from the men, they were confined inside an area fenced with bamboo. It was a prison inside a prison. This picture of the women exercising is not true to life; it was a "show" taken only for official propaganda.

One political prisoner sentenced to fifteen years named Yang Lao-chao was sent to carve "spiritual slogans" on the cliff behind the camp. A crowd at the top held the rope on which he was suspended as he worked, hanging in midair. After his job was done, he drew a comic of himself working.

F27

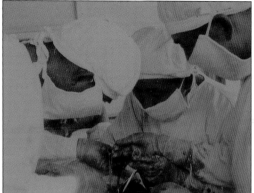

### Kenan ("Roughing It") Operation

In this early operating room, the equipment was rudimentary, without electricity. And yet many lives were saved thanks to the skill of the doctors.

### Political Prisoner Doctors

Many doctors were imprisoned or put to death during the White Terror. Doctors imprisoned on Green Island included representatives from practically every field of medicine, enough to staff a teaching hospital. Their patients included the political prisoners, the officers and soldiers at the camp, and the residents of Green Island. Dr. Su Yo-peng, *far left of the front now*, serving ten years, provided the photograph.

F28

### Class Notes

One woman named Chang Chin-chueh was sentenced to fifteen years. After doing her years in the Female Section on Green Island, she went back to Taiwan, where her imprisonment continued. This is the set of notes *Middle Eastern Situation and Military Strength* that she completed while at the Production Education Experiment Center in Tucheng, Taipei County in the 1960s.

F29

F30

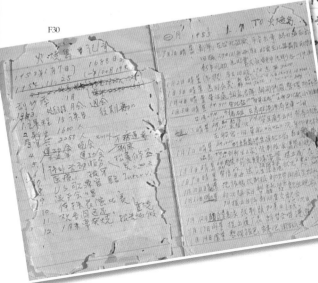

### Green Island Diary

One female prisoner named Chen Chin, who was sentenced to five years, covertly kept a diary while on Green Island and brought it back with her to Taiwan. This is a priceless first-hand historical document. Most political prisoners could not keep diaries, as the authorities conducted unannounced searches of their sleeping quarters, confiscating any materials considered suspicious.

# Prison Games

F31: A "marathon" of 5000 meters, for which prizes were awarded. The person on the far right is the renowned author and social activist Yang Kui. He was in prison twelve times in his life, the last time on Green Island, where he spent twelve years. He took part in the marathon at the age of fifty and was awarded a spirit prize.

F32: Volleyball Competition

F31

F33: Swimming Competition. The swimming pool was the men's bathing pool, the water for which came from Eel Ditch. The women had to carry water into their houses inside the fence when they wanted to bathe.

F34: The sports day was attended by almost all the men in the camp. Planned and prepared by the prisoners themselves, it was held seven times. This is the group photo of the Second Squadron at the Fourth Prison Games, taken on May 24, 1959.

F32

F33

F34

F35

F36

## Beijing Opera

One of the means of brainwashing, entertainment in the camp had to conform to official ideology. This is a picture of a Beijing Opera production, which was naturally performed by prisoners from the mainland. The picture at the right is Wang Hsiao-min, who often took the leading female role. She served twelve years.

## Taiwanese Folk Opera

Taiwan has its own opera, called Gezaixi. Gezaixi productions were put on by Taiwanese political prisoners. As the officers and soldiers at the camp were all mainlanders, the Taiwanese prisoners would often add in sarcastic dialogue when they were performing, producing unanticipated entertainment effects. For both Taiwanese and Beijing opera, the prisoners had to make the props and design the stage layout and backdrops by themselves.

F37

F38

## Formal Review

To accommodate senior officials or foreign visitors, political prisoners were occasionally gathered for formal "reviews," at which they had to declare their grudging loyalty to the authorities.

F39

## Physical Exercise

This picture was taken purely for propaganda purposes.

F40

## Foreign Visitors

It is as if they are visiting a zoo. Before the arrival of such guests, unruly political prisoners were separated, and those remaining were warned that no unauthorized interaction with the guest would be tolerated.

F41

## Official Visit

A group shot taken at the "Door to Revolution" Gate, probably so that the officials could enjoy the gratification of the elimination of political enemies.

## Celebrating Chiang Kai-shek's Birthday

Once every year during his reign as President of Taiwan, Chiang Kai-shek went to the extreme of requiring almost everyone on the island to take part in his birthday celebrations, even those he persecuted! No exception was made for political prisoners. This picture was taken in 1967 and was provided by Chen Meng-ho, *second from the right*. The Chinese slogan behind them is a birthday greeting to Chiang, reading, "Wishing that You Could Live Forever." Eight years later, when the birthday boy died, many political prisoners got reduced sentences or were released from prison.

F42

F43

### Political Assembly
Taken in 1954. The purpose of the occasion was to praise the virtues of Chiang Kai-shek. The command platform is made of reef rocks.

F44

### Searching for a Student
A National Taiwan University geologist, Lin Chao-chi, *second from the left*, doing fieldwork on Green Island takes the opportunity to ask political prisoner Chen Meng-ho, *left*, on the whereabouts of his student Yeh Hsueh-chun (sentenced to fifteen years).

F45

### Practice Band
There were many in the camp who had musical training and were well educated. They led their fellows in "roughing it" by making instruments so that a band could be formed in the camp. At the peak of activity, there were over 200 homemade guitars in the camp.

# Artefacts

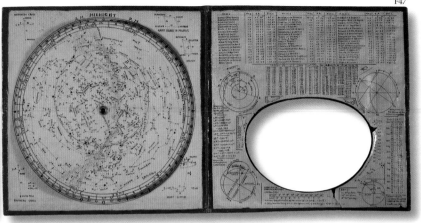

## Planisphaeria

The picture at the left is the outside; the picture at the right is the inside. This planisphaeria was done by the director of the ophthalmology department of the largest hospital in Taiwan, Dr. Hu Hsin-lin, who was sentenced to ten years. His son is the celebrated violinist Hu Nai-yuan. Green Island was where political prisoners had the least freedom but also where they could see the most magnificent and clear views of the heaventree of stars.

## Shell Paintings

This refined work of art was created by piecing together bits of shells and sea urchins. However, the main motivation was not artistic but material. Shell paintings were a monetary supplement especially for those political prisoners from the mainland, who didn't have family members to send them money. Either they sold them to the prison commissary or they gave them as presents to their fellow inmates.

## Diving Goggles

Made with a kind of softwood tree that grows on Green Island as well as found shards of broken glass, each pair of goggles was individually made-to-fit. Political prisoners working at the beach often scooped up seafood when not being watched as a way to supplement their diet.

## Homemade Violin

This richly toned violin was produced under incredibly difficult conditions. The front and back soundboards were made of the deckwood collected from a wrecked ship. The ribs were made using juniper wood from one of the camp buildings which had been blown over by a typhoon. The wood was softened by boiling and shaped in a mold. The neck and the bow were made from the handle of a hardwood hoe. The fingerboard and other parts were provided by inmate carpenters. The A string and E string were made of unraveled electrical cable, while the D string and G string were made of copper wire. The bowstring was made from tree root fibers. The violin case was made out of layers of glued fiberboard and was reinforced with a layer of material taken from prison garb. Chen Meng-ho spent the entirety of 1959 making this violin. In the life of the camp, there were over ten violins made this way in the face of adversity.

F50

## Translation of *Life of Jesus*

The Chinese translator of the original work by the Japanese humanitarian Yanaihara Tadao was Tu Nan-shan, sentenced to ten years. He worked in secret on this, the mainstay of his spiritual life. The original text was separated into ten parts and hidden in cracks in the wall in order to disperse the risk of confiscation. Luckily, the entire translation was brought back intact to Taiwan when Tu was discharged from prison. In 1986, after nine revisions, the Chinese version of the *Life of Jesus* was finally published.

F52

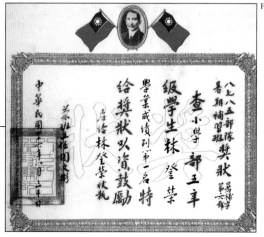

F51

## Certificate of Graduation

To felicitate relations with the Green Island residents, the camp would sometimes hold a "summer school." The political prisoners taught the local children, and when the classes were finished the kids would receive a certificate. For this reason, the political prisoners were highly respected by the local residents. When the children were asked what they wanted to be when they grew up, they would say, "New Lifer," the official name for political prisoners on Green Island.

Green Island During the White Terror II

# Oasis Villa (1972~1987)

In response to a February 1970 attempted uprising and breakout at Taiyuan Prison in Taitung, the KMT authorities swiftly built an enclosed prison on Green Island, called Oasis Villa, where inmates were subjected to severe military-style conditions—different from those at the earlier New Life Correction Center, in that the prisoners enjoyed far fewer activities. In addition, there were no official photographers to covertly send pictures as there had been before. This is why there are far fewer photographs of this incarceration center than of the earlier one, and why what photographs we must taken recently.

G1

### Prison Building

Political prisoners were confined in a four-wing two-story building. With wings radiating out from the center, this has been the typical prison design throughout the world since the 19th century. The first floors of the four wings were Areas 1-4, with Areas 5-8 on the second floors. Each area consisted of a long corridor with a row of cells on either side. There were in total 52 cells, in which at peak periods around 500 prisoners were confined, most of them concentrated on the first floors.

G2

Cells along the corridor

G3

Administration Building

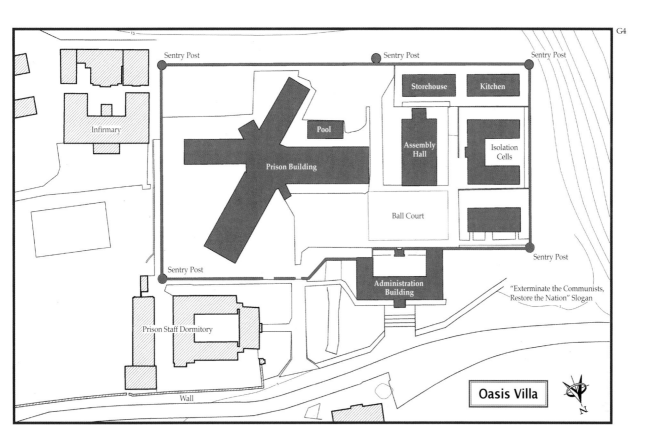

Oasis Villa

## Slogans
Etched on the mountain face and slopes, "Exterminate the Communists, Restore the Nation", *far right*, is representative.

G5

G6

G7

## Front Gate
The two-story building at the front right was the administration building, containing both the administrative center as well as a reception room, where political prisoners could meet with their families. The building now is the administration and reception center of the partly opened Green Island Human Rights Memorial Park.

Oasis Villa was once a place where unruly political prisoners were cruelly punished. Imprisonment might continue even after the prisoner's sentence had ended, without advance notice for the prisoner or his family. The political prisoner did not know what his fate was until the day he left the Villa: if he was taken towards the right after walking out of the prison gate, it meant release and freedom, but if he was taken to the left his imprisonment continued, even though there was no legal basis for it. The authorities extended sentences in this manner for up to three years.

re-enslavement        freedom

G8

G9

## Slogan on the Wall

The Oasis Villa wall was tall, with coiled barbed wire along the top. It once collapsed in a heavy rainfall, crushing one political prisoner to death. The slogan, *right*, reads "China Will Surely Be Strong." *Below*, "Resolutely Anti-Communist."

G10

G11

**Assembly Hall**
Now a gallery in the first phase of the Green Island Human Rights Memorial Park project. *(See page 165).*

G13

**Isolation Cell**
For the confinement of mental patients or "hard cases." Their hands and feet were manacled, leaving them no freedom to move.

G12

Prison Building Central Courtyard

G14

**Confinement Cell**
There are several isolation cells that were used to subject mental patients and hard cases to special treatment. These were the confinement cells, each of which had only a small opening at the top. Inside, it was pitch black, deathly lonely and suffocating, terrible enough to make a person go insane. The four walls of the cells were padded ten centimeters thick, to prevent prisoners from committing suicide.

G15

### Green Island's Last Political Prisoner

Wang Sing-nan, sentenced to life imprisonment in 1977, was always taking the lead in protests and in hunger strikes during his stay at Green Island (1977~1990). He fought for the right to increased activity time. After his release from prison, he was elected to the country's highest legislative body, the Legislative Yuan.

G16

Huang Hua, *right (see page 88)* and Yang Pi-chuan, *left (see page 4)*, both political prisoners advocating Taiwan independence, returned to Oasis Villa in 2002 for a visit.

G17

### Strolling on the Lawn

The grassy area around the four-wing prison building was for the prisoners to walk around on, for only fifteen minutes a day early on. Later, control was relaxed somewhat; the political prisoners themselves strove for increased freedom, so the daily free activity period was increased to a couple of hours. Prisoners could stroll around and were also permitted to play ball.

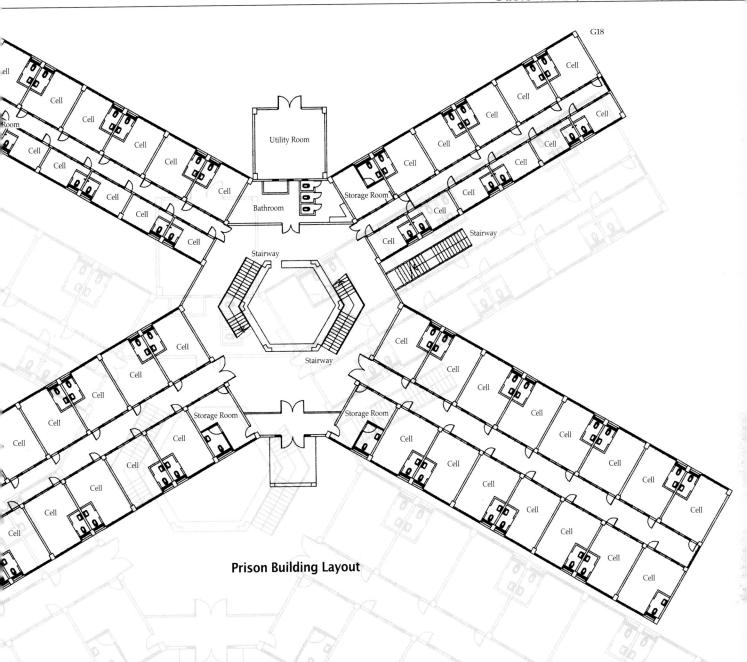

**Prison Building Layout**

## Shopping Coupons

Issued at Oasis Villa in 1972 for internal use only. The money sent to prisoners by their family was exchanged 1:1 for shopping coupons.

# Inmate Art Portraits of Prison Life

**But for writings and oral testimonies, there are few images
showing the circumstances of the different kinds of repression
suffered by political prisoners while in jail.
To make up for the loss, we have specially collected the works of several victims—
works based on their own true-life experiences.**

This painting by Ou Yang Chien-hua is based on what he saw with his own eyes while at the Martial Law Section Jail on Chingtao East Road. Several escapees were captured and brought back, after which they had their hands tied behind them and cloth stuck in their mouths and then they were strung up to be beaten, getting quite bloodied in the process. They were already half-dead after three or four days of this, and were taken out and shot.

(Painting by Ou Yang Chien-hua)

## Introduction to the Artists

### Ou Yang Chien-hua (1927~ )
*From Fuchien, he joined the Youth Army during the Sino-Japanese War, and then came to Taiwan with his unit. He was arrested for thought crimes in 1952, and was sentenced to three years of thought reform. Because he could find no guarantor, he served a total of over nine years before winning release.*

### Auyang Wen (1924~ )
*A native of Chiayi, he took part in the Chiayi armed resistance during the February 28 Incident. A student of political victim Chen Cheng-po, he was arrested in 1950 and sentenced to twelve*

*years. He is adept at painting and photography.*

### Chung Yi-jen (1921~ )
*Hailing from Taichung, he participated in the famed 27th Brigade military resistance during the February 28 Incident. Arrested in 1947, he served seventeen years in prison.*

### Yang Lao-chao (1924~ )
*A Taipei native, he was arrested the first time in 1950, and was sentenced three times, doing fifteen years. He's good at carving and painting.*

# General View of White Terror Torture
## Nineteen Tortures Suffered by Political Prisoner Yang Chin-hai

Yang Chin-hai (1932~) was a Kaohsiung businessman who in 1976 was arrested for advocating Taiwan Independence and organizing an opposition party. His original death sentence was ultimately reduced to life imprisonment only after people at home and abroad took up his defense, including three hearings conducted by US Congressman Stephen Solarz and an Amnesty International-led mobilization in which Chiang Ching-kuo was deluged by over thirty thousand telegrams. He was released in 1987. Held in a Bureau of Investigation prison in Ankeng, Hsintien, he was tortured for 57 days straight. Various implements were used. In 1984 he fled and through channels got information about his torture to Amnesty International. This was translated into five languages and distributed internationally.

1. Beatings: beaten with fists, elbows and arms, until his chest, back and legs were all black and blue, and he was spitting blood and had lost teeth.

2. Slaps: cheeks and neck were struck with the palm of the hand or a ruler until his lips and gums bled without letup.

3. Kicks: while wearing shoes they kicked him all over his body until his leg contusions were so bad that he could not walk.

4. Fatigue interrogation: each time the interrogation lasted three days and three nights, bringing on physical collapse.

5. Forced to crawl naked and make like a dog and bark like a dog: all the while they angrily cursed him and shouted abuse, and if they felt the slightest displeasure would hit him and kick him.

6. While naked kneeling down, holding both feet, and hopping like a rabbit: if he did not follow their cue, they would beat, kick and curse him.

7. Forced to smoke five cigarettes at the same time: knowing that he did not smoke, they stuffed five cigarettes into his mouth, until his nose dripped and eyes teared up; when the butts burned his mouth he was not allowed to spit them out. This went on for several hours, accompanied by curses and beatings.

8. Commanded him to kneel on bamboo sticks, chopsticks and ballpoint pens for hours: this continued until his legs were completely numb. Insults, curses and beatings all the while.

9. Commanded him to swallow a whole package of salt, with no water given him all day: only when he was allowed to use the lavatory did he manage to sneak some water from the toilet, resulting in long-term chest pain, numbness about the neck, fever, and difficulty in urinating.

10. While naked and with both hands tied behind the back and feet clamped securely, his mouth was stuffed with his own dirty underwear, and then he was beaten and kicked by five or six men.

11. Needles stuck into his fingertips: with both hands clamped securely, needles were thrust beneath his fingernails, and with two people holding him down, the person facing him questioned him while inserting the needles. If his replies did not meet their intentions, greater force was applied. Blood gushed forth, and his screams shook the heavens.

12. With both hands and feet cuffed, beaten to the ground, struck and kicked: bruises covered his body, and he could not move, so two guards had to carry him back to his cell.

H2

Yang Chin-hai, shown in front of the Presidential Building in 1989, as he participated in a demonstration to "Protest Oppression of the Foreign Regime, Demand Justice for All Political Prisoners." Lined up behind him are military police.

13. Finger press: with ball-point pens or small wood sticks placed between his fingers, pressure was applied, causing excruciating pain.

14. Stabbed with pen points: three or four pens were stuck in him all over his body.

15. Not allowed to urinate: not permitted to visit the toilet for several days running, there was nothing to do but pee in his pants.

16. Force-fed own phlegm and snot: he was made to eat everything he had expelled while being beaten.

17. Forced drinking of pepper-water: brought on recurring gastric ulcer and unconsciousness.

18. Kneeling on ice: this lasted for several hours.

19. Electric torture: while strapped to a chair, was wound up with telephone wire and electricity was applied—the telephone torture.

At the most, Green Island's New Life Correction Center held some one hundred women. They were locked up within a fenced enclosure that formed a prison within the prison. Not allowed out except for political activities and for fetching water, they could only do weaving and other such handiwork inside their barracks. A few of them were occasionally allowed out to attend stage performances.

(Painting by Ou Yang Chien-hua)

The New Life Correction Center held upwards of a thousand male political prisoners. Imitating the communist regime, the Kuomintang would foist upon them "labor reform to sap both mind and body." What tired one the most was gathering reef rock at the beach and carrying it back to build a wall and a bunch of sheds. Only primitive tools could be used, and there was no machinery.

(Painting by Ou Yang Chien-hua)

The inmates bathing together.          (Painting by Yang Lao-chao)

Auyang Wen was convicted in September 1950. He was sent to the National Defense Medical Center in October to serve as living experimental material in the teaching of dissection. They made a 15-cm incision in his belly without anesthetics, and a lot of male and female med students looked on as an organ was removed. After the operation, no painkillers were given, and when he cried out in pain, the doctor would only say, "Drink more water."          (Painting by Auyang Wen)

A cell at Taichung Prison                    (Painting by Chung Yi-jen)

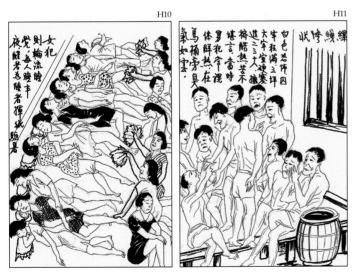

These two portray the inhuman treatment political prisoners suffered in their cells during the investigation period. The women's quarters were oppressively hot and crowded, and those awake had to fan the sleeping ones to keep the air moving. As for the men's cells, they were awash in body odor and the stench of urine and excrement. At right is a wooden bucket for removing the excrement of twenty to thirty people.                    (Painting by Ou Yang Chien-hua)

Taichung Prison

## Cruel Tortures Revealed in Book

Having been imprisoned twice (1964 and 1971), Hsieh Tsung-min's *Talking About the Martial Law Section Jail in Chingmei* is based on what he saw and heard while in prison. In the appendix there is a shocking list of tortures. The cruelty therein makes it a reprint from hell.

1. Plucking out of fingernails.
2. Finger press.
3. Tooth removal without benefit of anesthetics.
4. Pointed stick shoved up the anus.
5. Pepper-water forced through the nose.
6. Gasoline forced through the nose.
7. Force-fed lime.
8. Locked up in the iceroom.
9. Tied up and beaten savagely.
10. Hung from the rafters by both hands or both feet, beaten savagely.
11. Electric torture.
12. Put under a strong light.
13. Trip to hell: taken to the mountain cave to hear the cries of others being tortured.
14. Forced to drink urine.
15. Forced to eat dog feces.
16. Torture of the genitals.

These are but a part of the tortures regularly inflicted by the secret police, and there were others that were even more terrifying. Since China has known dictatorial rule for thousands of years, many tortures have been passed down from ancient times to the present, some of them causing death, or physical disorders that remain for the rest of one's days, like heart disease, deafness, crippling disabilities, and infertility.

Under militarized management, the New Life Correction Center issued inmates a stool to be used for classes and eating. The wood barracks were roofed with weeds, which rotted easily and were forever needing replacement, so weed-chopping on the mountain became a daily chore.
(Paintings by Ou Yang Chien-hua)

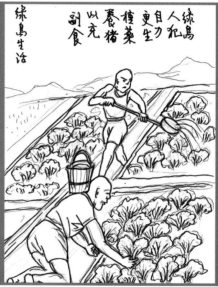

Political prisoners at the facility were treated like military conscripts. The rude pickings for food consisted of practically no vegetables. Overcoming all kinds of hardship, the freshmen were able to grow their own vegetables, and raise pigs and poultry. They were even able to grow enough to meet the needs of the officers and soldiers.
(Paintings by Ou Yang Chien-hua)

For their living, there were originally only a few wooden barracks to the New Life Correction Center. The inmates had to collect reef rock, and build a wall to pen themselves in (see note). They also built lots of sheds, to be used as warehouses and as the location for other activities.
(Paintings by Ou Yang Chien-hua)

*Note: This wall was playfully lampooned as the "Great Wall" by the political inmates. The hidden meaning was that the tyrannical rule of the KMT regime could be compared to the reign of the Chin Emperor (246-210 BC) in China.*

The "recreational activities" at the New Life Correction Center had to conform to the ideological requirements of the authorities. This was a running joke among those jailed for their "thought problems." Yet, setting up of the stage, making the props and singing and acting all provided yearned-for relief from tense, high-pressure living.

(Paintings by Ou Yang Chien-hua)

For the political inmates, most of whom were twenty to thirty years old, exercise, playing ball and swimming were the most popular activities. Water for the swimming pool came from Eel Ditch, Green Island's small creek and the New Life Correction Center's sole source of fresh water.

(Paintings by Ou Yang Chien-hua)

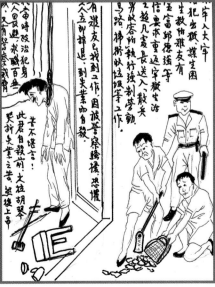

On the left is depicted the nabbing of a young man from a home where Mother has died, and the grief that has engulfed them. At right we see some former inmates who, having difficulty finding a job after release, demand to be sent back to prison, while another loses his job through police harassment, and ends up hanging himself.

(Paintings by Ou Yang Chien-hua)

H24~H30

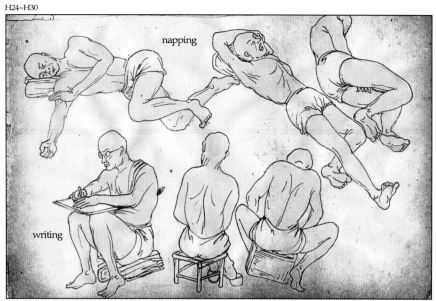

napping

writing

writing

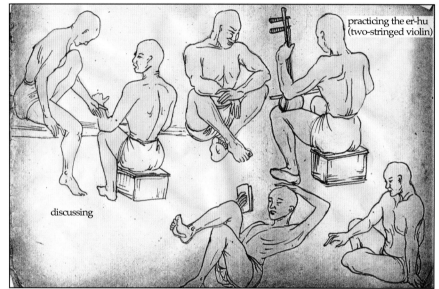

practicing the er-hu
(two-stringed violin)

discussing

reclining and reading

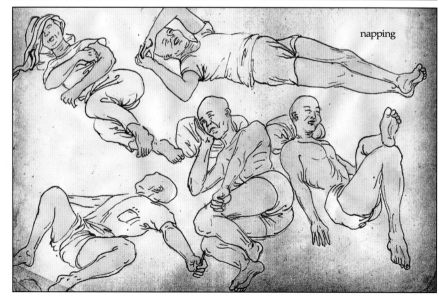

napping

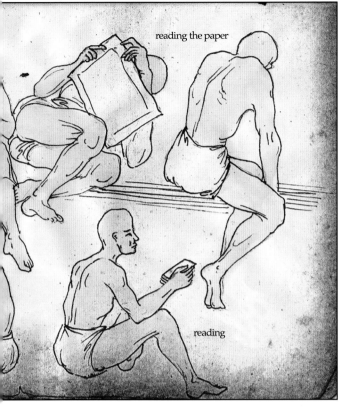

reading the paper

reading

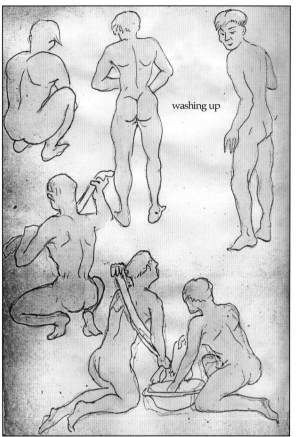

washing up

These sketches of daily life show how Ou Yang Chien-hua saw the daily leisure activities within the New Life Correction Center.

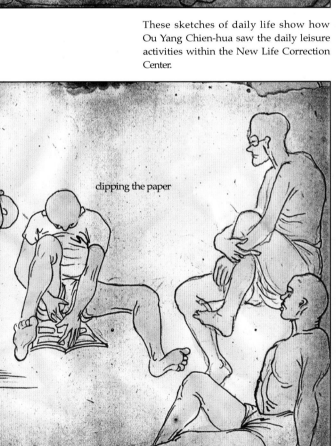

clipping the paper

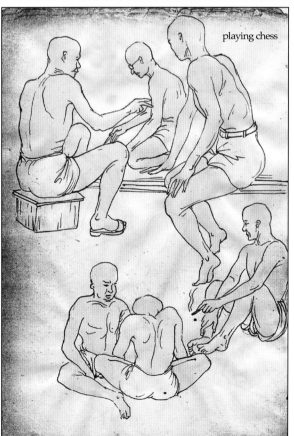

playing chess

# Prisons within Prisons

The dreadfulness of political imprisonment can be summed up in the expression, "The individual's criminality is calamity for the whole family; sitting in jail for a spell means a lifetime of hardship." The smaller prison involves the hardship of being locked up, while in the large prison one faces social ostracism. For the prisoners and their families, life-and-death crises were everywhere.

## The Vanished Population

In the 1950s, many political prisoners simply disappeared from their beds in the middle of the night, thereafter to lose all contact with their families. For many of them, the next time they would meet their family would be as an ice-cold corpse (see note 1). One former prisoner portrayed the experience perfectly as "an express ticket from bed to execution ground."

## Confiscation of Property

A cruel punishment awaited those who were sentenced to life imprisonment or death: all property, except for "considerations given to leaving what living expenses were needed by the family" were confiscated, the proceeds going to government coffers and as rewards to those who cracked the case (note 2). This regulation had the effect of creating a large homeless population. The victims lost their loved ones, their homes and their land, becoming destitute "political refugees" overnight.

## Supervision and Snap Inspections

After their arrest, both political prisoner and family came under the strictest supervision by the government authorities. Their daily activities were noted by the "cell," and reported up the line. Even after winning release, they were still subject to surveillance, snap inspections and harassment by the police and the secret police, or they had to appear at the local police station regularly to report on their comings and goings and on people with whom they had had contact. Some political prisoners were re-arrested many years after their release (note 3). Long-term persecution like this might last for thirty years and more—even after Martial Law ended in 1987.

## Families on Hard Times

Since the KMT were nothing less than obsessed when it came to those it accused of being "communist spies" or "rebels," they pulled out all stops to

I1

**Shih Shui-huan's letters to family**
Shih Shui-huan (1925~July 24, 1956) was a Telegraph Bureau employee hailing from Tainan. She was arrested for hiding her brother, National Taiwan University student Shih Chih-chen. Her brother escaped, and she was put to death.
This is a letter that Shih Shui-huan wrote to her elder sister two days before she was executed. The letter reveals the concern that she felt for her family, her last lines reading, "First thing every morning I read the Bible and pray. I pray for the grace of God."

I2

demonize the political prisoners; even the good names of their families were sullied in short order. Among some of the interconnected effects:

1. relatives and friends left off visiting their homes, and they were thrown into total isolation;
2. unable to bear the tragedy or difficulty of assuming the burden of the family's livelihood, their parents gave up waiting, and died before their release;
3. many of their spouses were driven to divorce, and some were even forced to marry the very secret police who were oppressing them;
4. their children often met with discrimination and ostracism in school, during military service and while job-hunting, putting them under a long-term cloud (note 4).

To give a rough estimate, families directly harmed by the White Terror account for at least 90,000 families.

Portrayed here we see harassment at the door of the political prisoner's family. Thanks to such visits, which were frequent, they had no peace day and night.

## Road to Employment Rocky at Best

Having forfeited their youth while in prison, the political prisoners were still to lose all kinds of job opportunities after release. The difficulties they faced included:

1. at time of sentencing, except where their prison time had already been served, they were often further penalized with loss of civil rights for several years following release (note 5);
2. there were at least 38 different professions—doctors, tour guides, professions that required certification, even midwives—for which it was stipulated that those with records of "rebellion" could not be employed;

This shows political prisoners (more often than not Mainlanders) who had no home to return to. They had to sleep on park benches, and in order to scrape together a living had to set up a sidewalk stand, meaning they were often bothered by the police.

### Husband-and-wife ex-con noodle vending team

Framed by secret police in November 1950, Nantou native Hung Chi-chung was sentenced to twelve years. Upon release, his work did not go smoothly thanks to harassment by the secret police. Later, he was able to scrape together a livelihood by means of a noodle stand operated with his wife, Chou Pi-hsia—herself a political prisoner sentenced to ten years. Through torture her backbone was beaten into a contorted shape, causing her lingering pain.

3. often the police or the secret police put pressure on the employers, forcing them to fire those with records of political imprisonment. Innumerable examples show that they could not manage more than a few days' work before being fired.

It should not be forgotten that many of these political prisoners were Taiwan's best and brightest young people. But they had now become marginalized, only able to work for meager pay or at jobs involving manual labor. They had no savings, no position, and typically remained poor into old age.

## Pain-wracked Body and Soul

Inhuman tyranny over body and soul through political imprisonment was in no way second to that of any other country under a rule of terror. A few examples will suffice to make the point.

1. Long after they had been released from prison, many political prisoners were still living in terror, fearing that any time they could be arrested again; since their personal dignity and sense of security had been destroyed while in prison, once released some prisoners could only pass their days in self-isolation.
2. Torture left many political prisoners with life-long disabilities, loss of their mental faculties, or permanent damage to internal organs.
3. Many of those released were to suffer from cancer and die prematurely, which, according to some former political prisoners, was related to the fact that over a long period they were fed on moldy rice and beans.
4. A number also had suffered physical and mental

hardships of various kinds, or upon release had difficulty earning a living, ultimately ending their lifelong suffering by committing suicide.

## Development of Another Type of Political Prisoner—1

Upon release, many of the political prisoners of the 1950s, 60s and 70s passed their days of hardship in quiet anonymity. There were but few exceptions, among them Hsu Yuan-tung (1927~1998), who was given three years of reform education for his part in the Keelung Work Committee, and would later go on to become director of first the Central Bank and later the Ministry of Finance. For his role in the April 6 Incident, Chang Kuang-chih (1931~2001) served one year in prison, but went on to become Taiwan's paramount archeologist and vice president of Taiwan's highest academic institution, the Academia Sinica.

## Development of Another Type of Political Prisoner—2

Up until 1989, the KMT regime did not relax in its arrest of political dissidents. After the 1979 Kaohsiung Incident, however, the popular conscience was reawakened, giving resolute backing to the opposition movement. This resulted in treatment of political offenders quite unlike that of before. Many prisoners were able to hold send-off parties before going to prison, with well-wishers numbering in the tens of thousands—in stark contrast to the 1950s, when political offenders simply vanished without a sound. Likewise after release, the latter-day prisoners

16

### Cheng Chiu-tu's letters
Cheng Chiu-tu (1926~March 26, 1952) was a train engineer from Hsinchu who was sentenced to death on charges of having belonged to the Taiwan Provincial Work Committee.
A month before his execution, he mailed a postcard to his son and daughter showing a hen and her two chicks peering at the cock, who is sitting in a cage awaiting slaughter.

17

祝 慶 元 宵

兒女健安

父 秋 徒 寄

2月P日

had their fortunes boosted upon release—president of the country, chairman of the DPP, legislators, county magistrates, many had backgrounds as political prisoners.

Elected president in 2000 and 2004, Chen Shui-bian went to prison in 1986 as part of the *Neo-Formosa* magazine case, and served eight months in prison. His vice president, Annette Lu, did eight years for her part in the Kaohsiung Incident case. Although the times and treatments given political prisoners differed, for their spirit of sacrifice for Taiwan, they should be accorded respect as comrades.

In 2000 Chen Shui-bian, *second from the left*, and Annette Lu, *left*, were elected as president and vice president of the country. Both having done time in the KMT's political prisons, they were reelected in 2004.

## Notes

1. *In the 1950s, in many cases the authorities did not notify the families of those who had been executed, but rather posted their names at Taipei Station. Afire with anxiety, the families would have to await word from the funeral parlor notifying them to retrieve the body—the first that they learned the dreadful news. But as for many of the victims who had come alone from the mainland, their families might never get word at all.*

2. *In certain cases, those getting ten-year sentences would also have their property confiscated. Since there were profits to be made in the confiscations, many secret police and court officers were only too happy to render the case all the more complex and serious, creating the most alarming wrongful imprisonments. Beneficiaries of the reward for cracking the case would include the government, informers, secret police, prosecutor, and judge. In some cases the money could be received in installments, just like a salary.*

3. *The most famous case of this kind was that of Chen Ming-chung, who was re-arrested in 1976. The case came about*

*because of some banned books, but was woven into a larger case so that a good number of former political prisoners could be nabbed a second time. The authorities had decided to execute two people in this case. Thanks to international pressure, however, the sentencing document was hastily revised, and seven people ended up getting seven to fifteen years.*

4. *In Taiwan, military service was compulsory for all males. Under close watch while in the military, the sons of political prisoners could not hold important posts, while it was virtually an open secret that the sons of the privileged class could escape military service or get off with lighter duties.*

5. *Those sentenced to life imprisonment or death were deprived of their rights for the rest of their days, while for those sentenced to lesser terms the period was somewhat less than the term of their sentence. This had the effect of shutting the victims out of political life for good, or at least for a long time, and was a way of guaranteeing the rule of the dictatorship.*

### Ke Chi-hua's New English Grammar

**Poet and teacher Ke Chi-hua (1929~2002), from Kaohsiung, was arrested once in 1951 and again in 1961, serving seventeen years in all. This *New English Grammar* was the most influential of English teaching materials in Taiwan, having sold about a million copies since 1960. Although there's hardly a high school student who has not profited from it, the book did not bear the name of its author for a long time because he was a political prisoner.**

# The Prisoners' Own Stories

## Elegies to Sufferings, Souls of Battles

**Native Taiwanese or Mainlander, pro-independence or pro-unification, leftist or rightist, it made no difference, for they all had a common, tragic fate in that absurd age. We present 24 stories as occasion permits. Here we will find humanity's hardships as well as the glory of the human spirit.**

### Chen Chih-hsiung (1916~1963)

Chen Chih-hsiung

Graduating from Tokyo Foreign Language University, this Pingtung native was assigned by the Japanese foreign ministry to Indonesia, then a Dutch colony under Japanese military rule. After the war, he threw himself into the Sukarno-led independence movement. Once Indonesia became independent, Sukarno began to tilt to Beijing, and had his erstwhile comrade-in-arms, the Taiwan Independence partisan Chen Chih-hsiung, thrown into jail.

Winning release, Chen continued to work as roving ambassador for Liao Wen-yi's Republic of Taiwan Provisional Government, and was very active in Japan. In 1959, the KMT dispatched agents to Japan to kidnap him, and he was secreted back to Taiwan by diplomatic pouch. At his sentencing in 1962, he said, "Alive I am Taiwanese, dead I will be a Taiwanese ghost." When he refused to kneel at his May 28, 1963 execution, his executioners hacked off his feet. Before dying, he loudly shouted, "Long live the Taiwanese people!"

### Fu Cheng (1927~1991)

Hailing from Jiangsu Province on the mainland, in his early years he was a model patriotic youth who "joined the army to repay the country." During short spells at two universities, his mind was opened up to the ideas of democracy and freedom. In 1953 he began submitting articles to *Free China*, the magazine begun by Lei Chen. In 1958 he began as the magazine's editor, later becoming its chief editor and Lei Chen's secretary. He was arrested in 1960 for participating in the movement to organize the China Democratic Party, and was sentenced to six years' imprisonment.

After the Kaohsiung Incident of 1979, Fu Cheng showed his concern for democracy by actively participating in the Tangwai Movement. At the establishment of the Democratic Progressive Party in 1986, Fu was one of the ten people in the Party Organizing Group, and was made responsible for organizational planning and drafting of important documents and declarations. He was the only one to have participated in the opposition's two organizing efforts, spanning thirty years.

Fu Cheng

## Green Island Lily (1944~1964)

1964 found trumpet-playing Taiwan Independence advocate Tseng Kuo-ying serving ten years at Green Island, where he joined the prisoner music group on its frequent tours around the island. Such tours put him on the same stage with a local beauty named Su Su-hsia. The two fell in love, their courtship incurring the jealousy of a political warfare officer named Liu *(see note 1)*. Poor Tseng was thereupon thrown into the pillbox, "Little Hell," and stayed there until the lady promised to marry Liu.

By promising to marry Liu, she succeeded in winning Tseng's release back into the larger hell. Once married to Liu, however, she denied him conjugal favors until, on an overnight trip to Taitung, she committed suicide—a triangular love tragedy in a gulag setting.

Su Su-hsia was another type of political victim.

## Hsieh Hsueh-hung (1901~1970)

Born to a worker family in Changhua, in 1922 she began to actively involve herself in the Taiwanese revolutionary movement. In 1925, with the support of the Third International, she went to the Far East University in Moscow, and had a hand in establishing the Taiwan Communist Party in Shanghai in 1928. Returning to Taiwan, she engaged in ceaseless struggle, both within and without, for the development of a Taiwan Communist force. By the end of the War in 1945, she had been arrested and imprisoned twice.

In the 1947 February 28 Incident, Hsieh was leader of the Taichung Militia. Once the incident ended, she fled to China, returning to Shanghai in November 1947. There she established the pro-CCP Taiwan Democratic Self-Government League, later holding such important positions as Political Negotiating Committee member. A bright woman of character, Hsieh subjected comrades to repeated "criticism sessions," just as she herself became a repeated victim of them.

During the Cultural Revolution on the mainland, Hsieh Hsueh-hung came under merciless Red Guard attack as an "important rightist."

## Hsieh Jui-jen (1909~1950)

A Tainan doctor who was providing free medical care to the poor, he was elected mayor of Matou Township twice, once in 1947 and again in 1950. His prospects grew brighter daily as he served the farmers enthusiastically during his terms, incurring the jealousy of his adversaries in the KMT. Nabbed in May 1950 as a "communist spy," he suffered especially savage torture and was executed on September 30, 1950.

His brothers had quite different fates. One of them, Hsieh Jui-chih was a high KMT official, won election to the national legislature and became principal of the Taiwan Police Academy. Another brother, Hsieh Jui-sheng, out of fierce love for his so-called ancestral county, went to China in 1932, where he went through the War of Resistance against Japan, the CCP-KMT civil war, and the Cultural Revolution. He was oppressed or deserted by the Japanese, the CCP and the KMT, each in their turn. In 1991, at the age of eighty, he returned to live in Taiwan but, six years later, was hospitalized, his long years of hardship having driven him insane.

Hsieh Jui-jen

## Hsu Chao-jung (1928~ )

Born in Pingtung, Hsu joined the Japanese Navy while young. Later, since the KMT military was targeting for massacre those Taiwanese who had done military service for the Japanese, he escaped by joining the military. Shortly thereafter he was dispatched to China to fight in the CCP-KMT civil war, then fled for his life back to Taiwan. Arrested for advocating Taiwan Independence in 1958, he served ten years, then, while in the US in 1986, became a political refugee when the KMT revoked his passport, whereupon he won political asylum in Canada.

In 1988, overcoming all kinds of difficulties, the sixty-year-old Hsu got heavily involved in a series of visits throughout China, where he sought out old Taiwanese soldiers and then fought with the KMT regime for their right to return to their homeland. After sticking tenaciously to his arduous duty, Hsu finally succeeded in the nineties, closing the curtain on what was for many old Taiwanese soldiers a forty-year diaspora.

In May 1985 Hsu Chao-jung, *left*, took part in events in Southern California supporting Shih Ming-teh, who was conducting a fast in prison at the time. His passport was revoked the following year. *On the right*, is the famous human rights activist, Linda Gail Arrigo, Shih's wife at the time.

## Hsu Hsi-tu (ca 1945~ )

In 1966 Taipei native and National Chengchi University graduate Hsu Hsi-tu was deeply moved by an article he read in the newspaper by an American student in Taiwan on the eve of his return to the US. The article expressed disappointment at the many corrupt aspects of Taiwan society. With a

Hsu Hsi-tu

strong sense of destiny, he roused many high school and university students to participate in movements for the public weal, and to use their youthful passion for service to transform society. In less than a year it had become an imposing youth organization attaining

considerable numbers.

The fast growth and size of this youth power lacking official sanction shocked the KMT, as it became a threat to Chiang Ching-kuo's China Youth Corps *(note 2)*. The arrests came in February 1969. Five young people were charged with "plotting to overthrow the government." Three were sentenced to life imprisonment, while one got ten years. The only one of the lot to escape punishment was Hsu: having been driven mad by the unbearable tortures, the only place deemed proper for him was the mental institution—which is where now, more than three decades later, he still remains *(note 3)*.

## Hsu Yueh-li (1912~ )

Heavily into socialist thought, the Taipei-born Hsu had already joined a left-wing organization by the age of sixteen through her involvement in the women's movement. She did volunteer work at a Taipei charity organization that exclusively catered to lepers and the indigent. In 1950, for having financially helped a political offender to escape, she was arrested and served twelve years.

At sixty she remarried to Chou Ho-yuan, also a former political prisoner. With the 1986 founding of the DPP, the couple became members, yet they left after finding their Taiwan-China unificationist thoughts did not accord with the party ideals, which stressed Taiwan Independence. Today, at ninety, reading socialist articles is her daily homework.

## Huang Hua (1939~ )

Native of Keelung, Huang graduated from the Naval Academy and then went to work at National Taiwan University. Rigorously self-taught, he was adept at law and English. He went to prison four times, first in 1963, when he did two-and-a-half years as a "gangster" after having stood for election. The second time

Huang Hua led this march, part of the movement for a new nation.

was in 1967, for having organized the National Youth Solidarity Promotion Association, which cost him seven years and ten months.

In 1976, after having served as the *Taiwan Political Review*'s deputy editor-in-chief, he was accused of rebellion and given eleven years. Upon leaving prison he joined the DPP, directing its organization department. At a time when the president of the country had yet to be chosen through popular elections, he was nominated by the DPP as its candidate. For promoting the New Nation Movement, which called for Taiwan Independence, he was imprisoned the fourth time, for ten years, of which he served a year and a half. Altogether he served nearly 23 years in prison. He's of genial temperament, laughs a lot, and is a true gentleman in the eyes of the people.

### Huang Tien (ca 1907~1950)

Born to a landlord family in Changhua, Huang was passionately loyal to the agrarian movement. He was a generous host, and so, for providing sanctuary for on-the-run members of the Taiwan Provincial Work Committee, seven members of his family, including his wife, sons, daughters and even a grandchild were hauled off to prison.

His daughter remembers seeing with her own eyes the heart-chilling spectacle of her father, after having been tortured. "With his whole body covered in blood and looking as if dead, he was dragged right past my cell." She fainted. Huang was one of fourteen people sentenced to death in the case, and was executed on December 19, 1950.

J9

Huang Tien's sweet home, with the male provider now gone, was made a family of calamity.

### Huang Ying-wu (1939~ )

After graduating from National Taiwan University, he returned to his native Ilan to teach. He organized the Taiwan People's Happiness Party in hopes

that with organized strength he could counter the KMT, maker of troubles. He was arrested in 1968 and sentenced to twelve years. He was given special treatment at the military prison in Hsintien: incarceration together with the mental patients for a half year.

There, in a special cell, were all kinds of people— the ceaselessly cursing, the shouting and jumping, the Jekyl and Hydes, the toilet cover tossers, and even those who would eat shit in front of everyone. In the midst of these lunatics, it was all Huang could do to keep himself from going mad. "In the first half of my life with all its darkness and dangers, nothing could compare to that period."

### Hung Shui-liu (ca 1916~1996)

A farmer from Tainan with no more than an elementary school education, he was implicated when in July 1950 the KMT arrested the Hsiaying Township mayor and a group of farmers on charges of belonging to the communist party. Sentenced to life, he was 35 when he went into prison. He served 33-and-a-half years, coming out at the age of 68.

The cruel tortures left a poisonous legacy of long-term health problems of many kinds, and, in August 1996, he committed suicide at the age of eighty. His last will read, "I am no longer able to bear the pain. Please restore me justice!"

J10

Hung Shui-liu, *second from right,* and his son and grandchildren photographed in front of their old home. By the time he was released from prison, Hung's father, brother and wife had passed away.

### Kao Chun-ming (1929~ )

A pastor from Tainan, Kao led the Presbyterian Church in Taiwan from 1970 to 1989, making him the longest-reigning secretary-general in the history of Taiwan's largest Christian denomination. During his term he succeeded in having the church issue three proclamations that went far in letting the call for human rights and sovereignty for Taiwan be heard around the world. In April 1980 he was arrested for harboring Shih Ming-teh, who was on the country's most-wanted

Rev. Kao Chun-ming, at a demonstration, 1988.

list for his role in the Kaohsiung Incident.

Kao bore his four years and three months of prison suffering and used the time to better himself, regarding his prison bars as if they belonged to a monastery. He read the Bible, intoned psalms, propagated the gospel, and helped many people to receive the faith and begin a new life.

## Leshin Wadan (Lin Jui-chang) (1899~1954)

Leshin Wadan

From the Indigenous Atayal tribe *(note 4)*, he graduated from Taiwan's one and only medical school in 1921, after which he returned to his native place to work, introducing advanced medicine and farming techniques to his tribe. He also actively sought the right of Taiwanese self-rule from the Japanese colonial government. After the war he was elected to the Taiwan Provincial Assembly, which at the time was the highest office held by an Aboriginal. Chiang Kai-shek, after his defeat in the CCP-KMT civil war, retreated to Taiwan in 1949, whereupon he holed up at Chiaopanshan in the mountains. There he was looked after by Wadan.

In March 1950 Chiang re-emerged, formally bringing Taiwan under his rule. It was then that the ensuing White Terror of the Chiang regime listed several Aboriginal young people of talent for inclusion in its massacres. In 1952, the authorities arrested Wadan, who had been struggling for Aboriginal self-

rule, as a communist spy. He went before the firing squad on February 23, 1954. Kao Yi-sheng, Tang Shou-jen and Kao Tse-chao were among the many talented Aboriginals who fell prey to the pogrom.

In October 1950, Chiang Kai-shek, *in long black overcoat*, paid a visit to his private villa in the hometown of Wadan, *left*. There were over forty such villas in Taiwan. *Second from the left* is Chiang Ching-kuo.

## Li Yu-tang (1900~1951)

A lieutenant general from Shantung Province on the mainland, Li had once commanded the Tenth Army, gaining fame for his part in the war with Japan (1937~1945). Awarded the Order of White Sun on Blue Sky, one of the highest honors conferred by the Chinese military, he had certainly done his bit for the KMT.

In September 1950, the KMT announced that it had arrested a communist spy. In October, on the pretext that the spy had had contact with Li, they arrested him too on charges of "concealing communist spy activity." On February 20, 1951, Li and his wife both went before the firing squad. Using the supporting actor, who is of dubious utility, to snare the innocent lead actor and have the lead actor take the rap was stereotypical among the methods frequently used by the KMT to liquidate "the big guys."

## Liu Ming (1902~1993)

After the war, Liu, a big-time miner from Chiayi who had the highest regard for education and culture, donating generously to the building and operation of schools, providing financial aid to artists, and helping a printing house out financially. In 1950, the said printer was discovered printing propaganda items for the Taiwan Provincial Work Committee, and Liu was implicated, thrown in jail, and sentenced to ten years. His considerable assets and a good number of buildings were confiscated.

While in prison, he regularly called on his family to send white shirts, to be worn by those who were to go before the death squad. He said, "The pure, clean blood of the Taiwanese must flow on a bright, clean shirt." Still today these words are passed on down by not a few former prisoners.

J14
Liu Ming and his wife

## Lu Chao-lin (1929~ )

In 1949, having taken up studies at Taiwan Normal College, this Changhua native was arrested for having taken part in the large-scale student movement, the April 6 Incident, but was released shortly after *(note 5)*. He was arrested again in November 1950 for having loaned banned books to a friend. Charged with having been behind a rebel organization, he was sentenced to life.

J15
Lu Chao-lin, photographed at the entrance to the Fifties White Terror Political Cases Redress Promotion Association, 2003.

After serving a quarter of a century in prison, he was released in 1975. He turned to organizational development for the Taiwan Political Prisoners Mutual Support Association *(note 6)*, which served society's weakest members, the former political prisoners. The group split in 1997, with Lu and others forming the Fifties White Terror Political Cases Redress Promotion Association, which sought to gain both financial compensation and restoration of justice for all political prisoners. Says Lu, "Human rights and democracy are equally important, and we should attend to them with all our strength."

## Lu Shui-ke (1917~1980)

An accomplished physician from Tainan, for some strange reason he was arrested in 1950, and the authorities accused him of playing a role in a rebel organization. Sentenced to ten years, he went to Green Island, where he often used night hours to meditate, while during the day when he was not working he would read.

He also went out on frequent medical calls to visit patients—from the prisoners and the surrounding villagers to the prison officials. If there were a medical emergency or serious malady, he was often sought out to deal with it. Released in 1960, he continued practicing medicine in his hometown. Doing time for him, it seems, was just so he could save that many more lives.

## Shih Yu-wei (ca 1926~1971)

From Jiangsu Province, Shih, a veteran Bureau of Investigation agent with a hundred-odd "rebellion" cases behind him, was described as "cunning and argumentative, with a deadly hand." In 1964, BOI chief Shen Chih-yueh began purging people from rival factions, and it is said that several hundred were taken in as communist spies, Shih Yu-wei among them.

This agent, whose stock-in-trade had been the handling of "communist spies," had now become one himself. He kept appealing each conviction, each time getting a heavier sentence, until, in 1971, he was executed together with seven others in the same case. Shortly before his execution, as if to demonstrate his innocence, he shouted at the top of his lungs, "Long live President Chiang!"

## Su Beng (1918~ )

A native of Taipei, Su has been a Taiwan Independence activist and determined Marxist. Graduating from Waseda University in 1942, he went to China, where he joined the CCP and warred with Japan. In 1947 he organized the 300-strong Taiwan Brigade to fight the KMT. It was at this time that he had to be on guard against the fearsomeness of Chinese nationalism and the humanity-obliterating methods of the Chinese communists, which gave rise to thoughts of Taiwan Independence.

J16
Su Beng

He returned to Taiwan in 1949, but fled to Japan in 1952 after a failed assassination plot on Chiang Kai-shek. There he remained for 41 years, while still carrying on with his planning of secret armed revolutionary actions within Taiwan. He also collected and researched copious historical materials, leading him to write *Taiwan's 400-Year History* (1962), which enjoys far-reaching influence and public recognition as a crowning work on Taiwan history.

## Tang Teh-chang (1907~1947)

His Japanese father died in the Chiaopanien Incident *(note 7)*. Tainan native Tang studied hard as a boy, and in 1939 went on to study in Japan, qualifying as a lawyer in 1943. Returning to Taiwan, he was chosen as chairman of the Tainan People's Freedom Protection Committee. He served

Tang Teh-chang

with enthusiasm, receiving the respect and adoration of others.

When the 1947 February 28 Incident broke out, Tang actively worked as negotiator between the authorities and the people. The situation rapidly stabilized, but once the KMT military arrived, he was falsely accused. Moreover, he refused to turn over to the military a list of those who had participated in the 2-28 uprising, and was executed on March 12. Thanks to acts of courage and principle like his, of any place in Taiwan, Tainan had the fewest number of people killed in the February 28 Incident.

## Tsai Tsai-yuan (1940~ )

Hailing from Kaohsiung, Tsai joined Shih Ming-teh in organizing the Asia League (forerunner of the Taiwan Independence League). In 1962 he was betrayed by an informer, arrested, and sentenced to twelve years.

While serving at the Martial Law Section Jail in Hsintien, he collected information on political prisoners from his fellow inmates, twice compiling lists which he passed through Hsieh Tsung-min and others into the hands of Amnesty International, which

In 1968, Tsai Tsai-yuan was jailed for a time at the MND Military Prison in Hsintien. This photo taken from the top of the jailhouse shows Block A, which was where Su Tung-chi was held at the time.

resulted in AI's publishing their Taiwan Human Rights Report, increasing international pressure on the KMT. Ultimately Tsai was tortured so badly that his spine became contorted, he was cuffed and shackled for six months, and three years were added to his sentence.

## Tsao Chao-su (1926~ )

From Hubei on the mainland, Tsao's father was Tsao Ya-po, one of the republic's earliest statesmen and major supporter of Sun Yat-sen's revolutionary movement, later to be assassinated by the KMT. In 1949 Tsao the son was nabbed and pressed into military service, coming with the military when it absconded to Taiwan. The following year he was arrested, tortured so badly that he was rendered infertile, and sentenced to twelve years for "participating in a rebel organization."

He says that actually he was sacrificed in the battle between Chiang Kai-shek's right-hand man, Chen Cheng, and Chiang's son, Chiang Ching-kuo. He was sentenced by Chen Cheng confidant Pao Chi-huang, head of the Ministry of National Defense Martial Law Bureau.

Tsao Chao-su, photographed beside the sea, Green Island

## Tuan Yun (ca 1906~1954)

J20

A lieutenant general from Hunan on the mainland, Tuan had commanded the 87th Army before coming to Taiwan to serve Chiang Kai-shek in several important posts, including vice commander of the Taiwan Defense Command. The commander there was Sun Li-jen, who, enjoying American support, was regarded by Chiang as a latent threat. Chiang wanted Tuan to "watch Sun Li-jen closely," and give him a report weekly.

According to observations, Tuan said frankly that Sun was loyal both to country and to the supreme leader, thereby incurring Chiang's wrath. Arrested in August 1950, he was executed on February 3, 1954. His brother and a cousin were both executed in the same case. While in prison, he told another friend-in-adversity that "I made no reports that violated my conscience, and this is something I am proud of."

Tuan Yun

## Notes

1. *These were cells assigned to the military by the KMT with the fine-sounding name of "political warfare." Nominally the New Life Correction Center belonged to the military, hence these cells. In the 1950s the KMT started copying the Soviets and the CCP by setting up a party section in the military, and assigned cells there to examine the officers' and soldiers' thoughts, and to force them to join the party. Controlling the military in this way was in open contravention of the constitution and the principle of putting the military under government control.*

2. *Founded in 1952, the formal name for the China Youth Corps was the China Youth Anti-Communist National Salvation Corps, with Chiang Kai-shek as its nominal head but in fact headed by Chiang Ching-kuo, who was director for 23 years. This was a means by which the KMT controlled and tamed young students. Military-style training, which came under the overall direction of the China Youth Corps, was offered at schools as a way of providing political education and thought-inspection of students in all high schools and universities.*

3. *By conservative estimates, there were at least several hundred political prisoners who, unable to withstand the torture and/ or incarceration, went crazy. The authorities built a prison in Tungshih, Taichung County, to specially accommodate them. Another place that has been revealed was a sanatorium in Yuli, Hualien County, with over four hundred political prisoners incarcerated there. Generally speaking, very few of the prisoners who went mad were rehabilitated and so were*

*destined for lifelong tragedy.*

4. *Long before the first Han people came to Taiwan, the Aboriginals had been here for several thousand years. Ethnically they are Austronesian, and are seen as the northern-most branch of this very extensive group. The Atayals are the largest of the twelve Aboriginal groups.*

5. *Regarded as the opening act of the White Terror, the April 6 Incident of 1949 was the first large-scale student movement of postwar Taiwan. Over two hundred students were arrested, the majority of whom were briefly detained and released, while others who had been involved in various political cases were incarcerated or shot.*

6. *"Mutual Aid Association" for short, it is seen as leaning to Taiwan-China unification, and is the second such organization of former political prisoners, the other being the Taiwan Independence-leaning Formosan Political Prisoner Association, established in 1987.*

7. *The 1915-16 Chiaopanien Incident took place in Tainan and featured the greatest number of dead and wounded of any event in the history of the Taiwanese resistance to the Japanese. After the Japanese lost several dozen colonialists, they exacted their revenge by massacring several thousand Taiwanese.*

# Historical Paper Legacy

## Documents from the White Terror (1949~1987)

### Who was behind the prisoners' executions?

Recently released official documents reveal that during the White Terror, political cases had their sentences decided not by the Martial Law Section of the Taiwan Security Command, but by the Ministry of National Defense (MND) Martial Law Bureau, Presidential Office and Chiang Kai-shek. It was especially Chiang who held the actual power over life and death. As the material makes clear, before sentencing, a "rebellion" case was sent to Chiang for review. The sentence would only be carried out after he had signed his approval and had his official seal affixed. What's more, for every political prisoner sentenced to death, two photos would be taken, one before execution, and the other after. Both would be sent to the Presidential Office for double-checking, to make sure that the person was in fact dead and would never return.

Should an ordinary citizen come under the accusation of "rebellion" at the time, nominally the sentencing would be handled by the secret Martial Law Section of the Security Command, but in fact political cases were treated the same as the military, all of whom would, in best military fashion, be put before the MND and Chiang Kai-shek, himself of warlord background. It was they who were responsible for the sentencing, and should someone become a prisoner in their hands, unlucky cases were sure to outnumber the lucky ones. Once the sentence had been announced, whenever someone was so fortunate as to get off with a life sentence, they would be treated to a fervent outpouring of congratulations from their fellow prisoners.

From official documents it can now be known that the process involved at least two steps. First, the Security Command's Martial Law Section sent a draft sentencing document to the MND's Martial Law Bureau. Then the Martial Law Bureau would forward its findings and recommendations to the Presidential Office, where Chiang Kai-shek would make the final judgment.

Review by the Martial Law Bureau and Presidential Office would often bring heavier sentence. Ordinarily, all such changes were accepted by Chiang.

Cheng Chieh-min

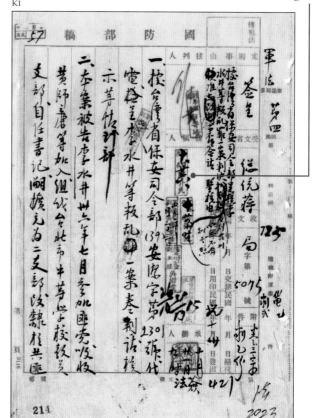

K1

In this MND submission to Chiang Kai-shek, views are explained concerning the draft sentencing of the Student Work Committee Case in May 1950. Of the seven people whose seals appear, one especially stands out—that of Cheng Chieh-min, who was the first to head the MND's Security Bureau as well as the first to head the National Security Bureau (which was in effect led by Chiang Ching-kuo). As for the roles that each of the Chiangs played, to put it simply, it was the father's responsibility to pass judgment, while the son had charge of arrests.

per recommendation

Chiang Kai-shek's seal

Those arrested in connection with the January 1950 Taipei Work Committee Case and the May 1950 Student Work Committee Case were all leading intellectuals of the day. In the original sentencing draft for the SWCC, only five people were sentenced to death, but this submission, *right*, by the Presidential Office to Chiang Kai-shek recommends that six people have their life sentences changed to death. With Chiang's simple "per recommendation," in a wink the number of those headed for execution doubled. Likewise, of the TWCC defendants in this review document, *left*, four people (three of whom were originally sentenced to life, one to eighteen years) had their lives taken from them by this secret tribunal.

## Postwar Financial Crisis

After the war, with the incoming KMT regime of Chen Yi engaged in rampant corruption and robbery, commodity prices took a big jump and the financial markets fell into chaos *(see note 1)*. On May 17, 1949, three days before Martial Law was declared, the Taiwan Provincial Police Section publicly announced that illegal underground moneychangers would be policed. They also announced that those "few businesspeople" who displayed prices in gold, U.S. dollars or silver coins would be banned.

At the time there were over five hundred underground moneychangers in Taiwan. They had taken the place of the banks, whose trust had been bankrupted, and had become fearsome sponges of capital *(note 2)*. Against the backdrop of the war between the KMT and the CCP still raging on the mainland, the depressed business situation gave rise to widespread interest in socialist thought and helped plant the seeds of still more tragedy to come in Taiwan.

## Wang Sheng-ho and Li Peng

On March 1, 1950, the KMT authorities announced that they had cracked a case of Soviet spies operating in Taiwan. Charged with having set up a secret broadcasting station and supplying intelligence to the GPU in the Soviet Union were Wang Sheng-ho, *left*, a radio engineer, and Li Peng, *right*, reporter for the *New York Times* and *Time* magazine. Four people—Wang Sheng-ho and his wife, and Li Peng and his lover—were sentenced to death, and eight people got prison sentences ranging from seven to ten years. Not only did this accord with the "national policy" of "opposing communism and resisting the Soviets," but it also signified a trade-off for US support.

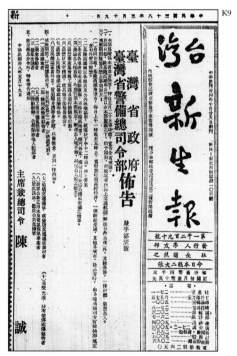

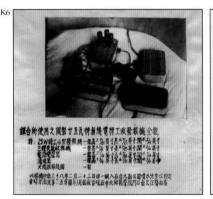

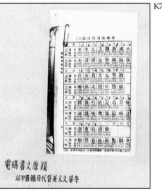

## Communication Equipment Used by Wang Sheng-ho and Li Peng

*At left*, the small 2.5-watt wireless transceiver was the one used by Wang and Li's station. *At right* is shown their secret codebooks. The code system utilized numbers, English letters and Chinese phonetics in a comparison table, which was extremely complicated and difficult to crack.

## Martial Law Decree

On May 20, 1949, Taiwan entered what was to become the world's longest-running period of martial law. During 38 years, marches and petitions were strictly forbidden. Whether you were at home or outside, you had to carry your national ID at all times, on pain of arrest *(note 3)*. "Spreading rumors," "misleading the public," and "mass riots" were among the crimes punishable by death. This drawing is from the *Hsin Sheng Daily News*, whose publisher, Li Yu-pang, was a victim of the Martial Law decree. On April 22, 1952, he was executed for "rebellion."

K10

K11

### Statutes for the Detection and Eradication of Spies During the Period of Communist Rebellion

Promulgated on June 13, 1950, these required that everyone serving in private companies, in the military, at schools or in factories had to have at least two personal guarantors. If the person being guaranteed were charged as a "communist spy" (a charge that might be wholly fabricated), the guarantors would also be punished. Another article in the law decreed that anyone knowing about a "communist spy" and not reporting him or her, would also be punished. The meaning was clear: in order to protect yourself, you had to disown your own relatives. This all-encompassing legal instrument of terror destroyed honesty and trust on the individual level.

### List of the First Group of "Undercover Communists"

Through the mass arrests of the 1950s, the authorities liquidated many "communist spies." On November 17, 1951 the Taiwan Security Command issued orders for the arrest of undercover communists that had not surrendered. The vast majority of them were nabbed, and by 1954 the membership of the Taiwan Provincial Work Committee had been completely wiped out.

### Formosa People's Self-Rescue Struggle Youth League Case

The case broke on August 16, 1952, and was cracked by the Defense Ministry's Security Bureau. This document is a report submitted to the Executive Yuan by the Security Bureau. In this, a model aboriginal political

K12

case, their leader, Lin Chao-ming, was the nephew of Atayal chieftain Leshin Wadan (Lin Jui-chang), executed in another case. Lin Chao-ming had gotten together some aboriginal students from normal college to organize a youth alliance to petition for tribal awareness, self-rule, and self-defense. Three people were sentenced to fifteen years in the case, while five more got two to seven years. The authorities continued to "disinfect," and arrests continued for another twenty years, as did the arrests of other aboriginal normal students.

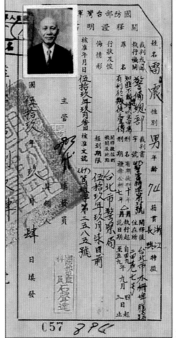

K13

### Lei Chen Document I: Military Prison Releases Document

From this document, drawn up on September 4, 1970, can be seen that Lei Chen was 74 at the time. His "crime" was to have "repeatedly disseminated words benefiting the rebels," an obvious reference to *Free China*, a liberal magazine that he founded.

K14

K15

K16

### Release of Lei Chen Document II: Letter of Guarantee

When political prisoners were released, they needed two or more guarantors, an international joke. Lei Chen's letter of guarantee is an example of two guarantors being held responsible for the subject's "fidelity to the Three Principles of the People, obedience to the government's commands, and receptiveness to specified work and directives." They also take responsibility for the subject's livelihood, words and actions, and have to report all these to the police monthly.

Issued in 1953, the registration certificate for *Free China* shows Lei Chen, then aged 57.

## Notes

1. From 1946 to 1951, Taiwan's average commodity prices jumped 9600 times. In early 1949, when Taiwan's population stood at six million, there were between 400 and 800 thousand people unemployed. This was colossal economic terror, and it was not until after the issuing of the New Taiwan Dollar in June 1949 and the beginning of US aid in 1951, that the situation slowly began to improve.

2. Two kinds of damage to Taiwan's economy were incurred because of the civil war between the KMT and the CCP: vast Taiwan material treasure was stolen and shipped off to China to fill wartime requirements, and massive amounts of liquid assets on the mainland were removed to the safety of Taiwan, there to be invested and used in manipulative transactions. The result was greatly accelerated inflation. With prospects for profitmaking so hopeless, all the Taiwanese could

do was put their money in underground money-changing, which offered the enticement of higher rates. But soon after, policing of the moneychangers began, with many going belly-up, and Taiwanese by the thousands became victims of the financial storm.

3. The national ID originally came about during the war between China and Japan on the mainland (1937~1945). Invented by the Japanese military as a system to control Chinese in the areas under occupation, it was continued by the KMT to rule the Taiwanese. A most efficient means of population control, the ID carried basic information on every individual fourteen years or older, and had to be produced by the bearer at every important occasion in life, from securing new employment to changing his or her place of residence.

Painted by Auyang Wen

# Reborn

Abundant and hardy, the Taiwan lily (*Lilium formosanum Wallace*) is a symbol of the Taiwanese spirit. You can see it on Green Island. It grows with fiercest pride right up alongside the prison blocks, as a witness to the recurring cycle that plays through Taiwanese history: victimization, resistance, and rebirth.

# The Great Taiwan Massacre

## March~May 1947

"Terror Inspection," a woodblock print depicting the February 28 Incident by Huang Jung-tsan, who died in the White Terror on November 14, 1952.

The Japanese defeat in World War II marked the return to Chinese rule of Taiwan, which had been under Japanese control since 1895. On October 25, 1945, the Taiwanese people welcomed with patriotic fanfare and anticipation the arrival of Chen Yi, the newly appointed administrator under Generalissimo Chiang Kai-shek. However, this historic reception became the ironic beginning of another poignant epoch in Taiwanese history. During the postwar period, the alarming rate of inflation and unemployment aggravated economic collapse and social malaise. Public support and confidence in the new administration were ultimately eroded by government corruption. The sequence of events collectively known as the February 28 Incident began in Taipei on the night of February 27, 1947. A female vendor pleading for her confiscated tobacco was beaten by the tobacco monopoly agent, who then fired into a crowd of emotional onlookers, accidentally killing an innocent bystander. The turning point took place the next day as the public demonstrations abruptly ended in more random shootings by the police.

Beginning March 1, people stood up everywhere across Taiwan in an outcry for justice and political reform. Consequently, Chen Yi appointed a reconciliatory February 28 Incident Committee to appease the public. While this committee of government representatives and local leaders was reaching a resolution, Chiang Kai-shek responded to Chen Yi's request by dispatching armed troops to Taiwan. The infamous 21st Division landed in Keelung on March 8 and, following orders for the "Countryside Cleanup" campaign, began the bloody massacre across the island. Among tens of thousands of innocent victims were prominent leaders, educators, officials, journalists, and former members of the February 28 Incident Committee.

*(The above is adapted from the "Introduction to the February 28 Incident," by the Taipei 228 Memorial Museum.)*

The February 28 Incident is the name given to the conflict surrounding the confiscation of contraband cigarettes on February 27, the protest movement that followed it and lasted for about two weeks, and the two months of massacre all over Taiwan. In the hearts of the Taiwanese, it was another way of saying "bloody death."

The great massacre of 1947 was but the opening act in a post-war tragedy lasting half a century. A mere two years passed before the White Terror came on stage to continue adding to the island's scars. It was like a black hole, ceaselessly sucking the politically repressed, of whom the vast majority were innocent, into destruction.

So as to present an in-depth, more concrete introduction to the 1947 massacre, the editors have chosen just a sampling, selecting nine massacre locations and choosing several individual recollections to illustrate them. These recollections are taken from a series of books collecting the oral histories of the participants.

This descriptive method offers the perspective of "human rights suffering" to enable us to understand the many different types of repression suffered by humanity. We can understand that in the February 28 Incident, a human life was no more than that of an ant, and it helps us to realize the extent of the chill and sorrow of the White Terror.

## Keelung's Sea of Blood

Upon landing at Keelung on March 9, the Kuomintang troops began their wholesale slaughter, firing on the unarmed populace indiscriminately, or running steel wire through their victims' palms and ankles and then sweeping them with machinegun fire, after which they would be thrown in the sea until the Keelung Harbor was covered with floating corpses. The once-beautiful harbor became a red sea full of stinking corpses.

### Chen Chao-hui

Assistant engineer in a Keelung coal mining operation, on March 14 he was taken away by some soldiers claiming that they were from the electric company. Thereafter his whereabouts became unknown. His family found him two weeks later, by which time he was a floating corpse in the ocean, so swollen that he could barely fit in the coffin.

*Chang Pi-yu (the deceased's widow): "When we fetched his body, he was blindfolded with Japanese military spats, and cotton cloth had been stuffed into his mouth. His hands were tied behind his back. His feet were bound with wire. Planning to hide the body, they bound him to a rock so that his body* would not float, and stuffed something in his mouth so he could not call out." *(From* Rainy Harbor Keelung, February 28, Independence Evening Post, *1994.)*

### Lin Mu-chi

A worker with the Keelung Police Bureau, he was taken away for no apparent reason by three policemen after the outbreak of the February 28 Incident. Mercilessly tortured, by some miracle he was rescued from the hands of death, but still today his hands, the palms of which were strung through with steel wire, still ache and have no strength.

*Lin Mu-chi: "We were bound up into nine rows, with nine people in a row. About a hundred or more troops started binding us up with steel wire, and blindfolding us with rags. Not long after that, I heard the sound of continuous gunfire. Later I discovered that it was the eight people in front of me who saved my life. After they were shot, one by one they fell into the sea, and I was dragged down. After entering the water, I felt the steel wire that bound my legs loosen, and I managed to escape with my life." (From* Rainy Harbor Keelung, February 28, Independence Evening Post, *1994.)*

# Tragedy at Patu Station

On March 1st, some soldiers boarded a train at the northeast tip of Taiwan and headed for Patu Station. Since a section of the track had been destroyed during wartime air raids, the train could proceed no further and stopped so that the passengers could board a second train. The military, however, angry at the failure of the train to move forward, came into conflict with the people. On March 11 they took revenge, shooting five to seven workers, and arresting another eleven who had been working on March 1st. The eleven were never found.

## Hsu Chao-tsung

Deputy station master at Patu Station, after going to work on March 11, he was never seen again.

*Hsu Chiang-chun (widow of the deceased): "There were lots of bodies floating on the ocean in Keelung. You could hardly make out their faces. We went to identify the bodies one by one, and I had to go by the clothing to tell whether it was my husband. One time when I went to identify the corpses, I looked forever but couldn't find him. I stood there all alone by the sea, and, thinking of my situation, wanted to jump in the sea and kill myself." (From* Train Station of Sorrow, February 28, *Independence Evening Post, 1993.)*

Huang Jung-tsan's gravestone, discovered in Liuchangli

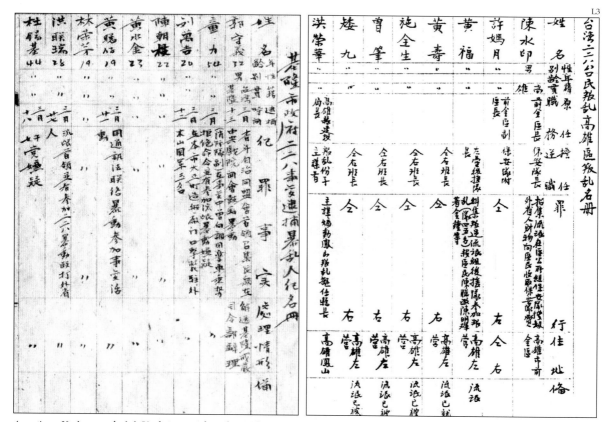

A portion – Keelung on the left, Kaohsiung on the right – of the arrest list made up by the authorities in response to the February 28 Incident . For their suspected involvement in the incident, many of them were executed.

# Taipei Hell

The most tragic deaths of the February 28 Incident occurred in Taipei. Realistic portrayals of the city of that time were like descriptions of scenes from hell, like the copse of hanging corpses at Yuanshan, the streets flowing in blood, the decapitations, and the abnormally cruel killings. Carload after carload of bodies were transported to the Tamsui River that flowed through the city, where they were dumped, "causing the normally yellow Tamsui River to turn red, with the rotten corpses floating on the top. The scene was so sordid that no one could look on it." (From the famous work describing the February 28 Incident, *Angry Taiwan* (1949), by Su Hsin, a leftist who escaped to the mainland after the incident.)

## Chen Neng-tung

Principal of Tamsui Middle School, which was run by the Formosa Presbyterian Church, he was arrested without reason on March 11, and was never seen again. The school's first principal and Taiwan's first PhD in philosophy (from Columbia University), Lin Mao-sheng was also a victim of the February 28 Incident.

Chen Neng-tung

*Chen Ying-chi (son of the deceased): "At a little after seven in the morning, someone came knocking at the door. They didn't say anything, but came rushing into the house and forced Father out of bed. He wasn't allowed to put on his clothes or shoes, and was taken away. Some said that he may have been shot at Keelung and thrown into the sea, while others said that he may have been beaten to death at Nankang. In the end we didn't know what became of him." (From* Tamsui Watershed, February 28, *Wu San-lien Historical Materials Foundation, 1996.)*

## Lin Li-chiang

A student at National Taiwan University, after leaving his sister's home on March 8, he was never heard from again.

Lin Li-chiang

*Lin Li-shan (sister of the deceased): "I searched high and low for him. On the river there were lots of bodies floating, some of them headless, some with their eyes popped out, others missing hands and feet, while still others were naked. Even before you got to the Botanical Gardens, a tremendous stench assaulted you from afar. All kinds of terrible deaths there were. After my brother disappeared, I kept waiting for him to appear. But one year came and went, then another, and still no news. Right up to the past few years, with myself getting old, I've finally given up hope." (From* The Taipei Capital, February 28, *Wu San-lien Historical Materials Foundation, 1996.)*

## Chiu Shou-yang

After the outbreak of the February 28 Incident, on March 9, Chiu, a teacher, went to the military to protest that soldiers were scaring the vendors by buying food at gunpoint. The day next he was arrested and shot.

*Chiu Chen-hsueh (widow of the deceased): "When we dug him out of his grave, gone were my husband's suit jacket and coat. All that was left was his trousers. His body was riddled with bullet holes. Once he died, many people would have nothing to do with us." (From* Tamsui Watershed, February 28, *Wu San-lien Historical Materials Foundation, 1996.)*

## Sung Fei-ju

He was the president of *People's Report*, a newspaper resented by Chen Yi for its attacks on government corruption. He was arrested in March, never to return. Wang Tien-teng, who took over from him as president of the paper, was also arrested, and died a flaming death after being doused with gasoline by MPs. Sung's widow, Ou Yen-hua, died in the White Terror of 1949.

*Sung Hung-tao (son of the deceased): "I was 16 years old when these things befell my father, and immediately everyone was cold to us and relatives kept their distance. After Father died, his body was never found, but I am sure that he died, because he had 'appeared' to us." (From* The Taipei Capital, February 28, *Wu San-lien Historical Materials Foundation, 1996.)*

Father and son, Sung Fei-ju and Sung Hung-tao

# Nankang's Eight Corpses

In the middle of March, in Nankang (eastern Taipei), the bodies of eight people who had died miserably were found beneath a bridge. Of the five who could be recognized, one was the body of Wu Hung-chi, who was from the family of Wu Po-hsiung, now the vice chairman of the Kuomintang.

## Wu Hung-chi

A prosecutor with the high court, perhaps it was because he was upright in his handling of cases that he upset the authorities and fell victim in the February 28 events. His widow, Yang Chao-chih, found his body under a bridge in Nankang, and had a photographer shoot a picture of her husband's corpse.

*Yang Chao-chih: "His coat was missing, as were his watch and shoes. We took his body home, and once we got into the house, he began bleeding without letup. He had wounds all over his body, and even his testicles were crushed. In the* Book of Romans, *Jehovah says that justice should be sought in Him, and He will manage retribution. In this have I sought solace for these decades,*

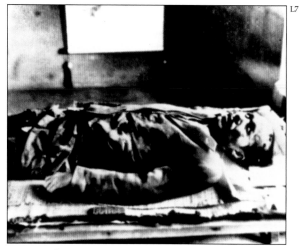

Wu Hung-chi's body

*that is the strength of this saying. One day justice will be done."* (From Taipei-Nankang, February 28, Wu San-lien Historical Materials Foundation, 1995.)

# Death Hills in Yunlin-Chiayi

After the outbreak of the February 28 Incident, people formed militias in Yunlin and Chiayi to defend the country. When the situation changed, they removed to the hills in March, but many of them were killed when ambushed at Kukeng by KMT troops. A half a century later, in November 1997, an expert task force began excavation work at Kukeng, and in the first day dug up thirteen bodies.

## Hsu Jen-chen

A clerk with the district court, he helped organize the militia in Yunlin, succeeding in repulsing an attack on the city by the KMT troops. To avoid civilian casualties in the city, he led the militia out into the suburbs, where he was ambushed. He was bayoneted to death.

*Lin Yu-ying (widow of the deceased): "A Mainlander, the mayor of Chiayi feared getting beaten by the Taiwanese. My husband protected him and sent him off to live in our dormitory. He said that the mayor was a good man, not corrupt, and would never cheat the Taiwanese. My husband captained a militia company and went off to the mountains with a hundred of them, but fighting broke out with the soldiers en route, and he was killed, and buried in a pit together with 28 others." (From Yunlin-Chiayi, February 28, Wu San-lien Historical Materials Foundation, 1995.)*

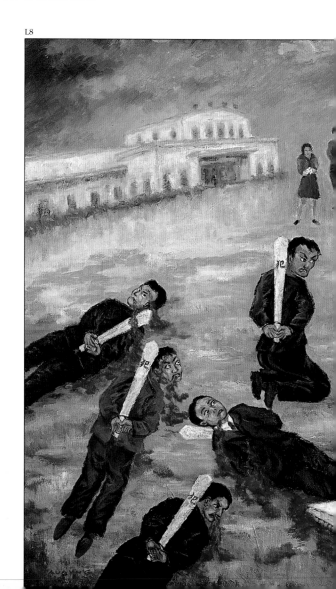

# Public Executions, Chiayi Station

On March 12, the KMT troops entered Chiayi City and began mass arrests. On March 25, militia leader Chen Fu-chih, painter Chen Cheng-po, city councilmen Pan Mu-chih and Ko Lin, journalist Su Hsien-chang and others were tied up and paraded around the city, and then taken to the front of the railway station, where they were publicly executed and their bodies put on display.

## Chen Cheng-po

A Chiayi city councilman, Chen was one of Taiwan's most talented early-period painters.

*Chen Chung-kuang (son of the deceased): "After Father was shot, Mother insisted on taking a picture of his body. A few months before she died, all her terrors came forth. When a guest came calling, she was very ill at ease, and would ask me, 'Isn't it a bad guy that's come?' And sometimes she would say, 'Your Father has been arrested. Hurry! Go and save him! What are you sitting there for?' She was unable to control herself."* (From Chiayi Station Plaza, February 28, *Wu San-lien Historical Materials Foundation, 1995.*)

## Lu Ping-chin

A dentist and city councilman, he tried to rescue other city council members who were being detained, and was himself arrested.

Lu Ping-chin

*Lin Hsiu-mei (widow of the deceased): "We heard that at noon on the day that they were executed, nobody in all of Chiayi ate lunch.... The night after he was shot, his spirit came back, and spent the whole night in our backyard crying.... He was shot because he had been collecting information on corrupt officials.... I gave his behavior the highest affirmation by inscribing on his tomb, 'Dead before history.'"* (From Chiayi Station Plaza, February 28, *Wu San-lien Historical Materials Foundation, 1995.*)

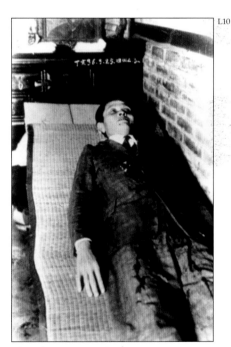

Chen Cheng-po's body

In this oil rendition of the shootings in front of Chiayi Station, the 228 Memorial Plaque commemorating this tragedy can be seen at the center.

(Painting by Auyang Wen, a student of Chen Cheng-po)

L11

# Kaohsiung Blood Rites

During the February 28 Uprising, with the exception of the military base at Shoushan, all around Kaohsiung City, government agencies were under the occupation of the people's militia. On March 5, commander of the base, Peng Meng-chi, shelled the city to terrorize the people. The next day, five people led by Kaohsiung mayor Huang Chung-tu went to negotiate with Peng, and were arrested on the spot. That afternoon, Peng sent troops down the mountain to begin a massacre in the city, with the command that they should kill on sight, while at the same time calling on reinforcements from troops garrisoned at Fengshan. The massacre continued until the eighth, as bodies kept piling up in the city. The stench and bloody scenes made it seem like the end of the world.

## Madam Chang Pu

On the morning of March 7 she took a bullet in the belly while carrying her four-year-old son, Liang Chin-chung, through the city. So as to protect her son, she forced herself to walk back home for medical attention, but died the next day.

*Liang Chin-chung: "After Mother died, Father didn't have the money to take care of matters, and so the coffin was just thrown together from some wood planks, and she was hastily buried in a public cemetery which was later abandoned, so that Mother's grave could not be found." (From* Dove of Peace No. 1, *Taipei 228 Memorial Museum, 1997.)*

## Lin Chieh

L12

A ward captain, he was one of the five who went to see General Peng Meng-chi. He was tied up, and then shot from behind.

*Lin Li-tsai (daughter of the deceased): "I was two years old when Father died. Mother, who was in extremely great pain and terror, and unable to take the long-term strain, killed herself when I was nine." (From* Dove of Peace No. 1, *Taipei 228 Memorial Museum, 1997.)*

Lin Li-tsai and father, Lin Chieh

Liang Chin-chung, seen holding the sign and pulling an artificial corpse, participated in the February 28 commemorative march; the sign reads, "Mother, where are you?"

# The Fenglin Tragedy

Chang Chi-lang and his three sons, Chang Tsung-jen, Chang Yi-jen, and Chang Kuo-jen, were all famous doctors in Fenglin, a small town in Hualien on the east coast of Taiwan. After the war, Chang Chi-lang enthusiastically started preparing for the arrival of the new government, and was elected speaker of the Hualien County Council as well as representative of the National Assembly. For no reason he and his three sons were arrested on April 4. Thanks to documents carried on his person, proving that he was a military medic, Chang Yi-jen was spared, but the other three were taken outside the town and shot.

*Chang Yu-chan (widow of Chang Kuo-jen):* "At the time, it was not yet dark, so I didn't dare bring the bodies back, and it was not until April 6 that, before morning light, I was able to fetch them with an ox cart. Each of them had been shot twice, and my husband's guts were spilled out." (From Women's February 28, *Taiwan Interminds Publishing, 1997*.)

# February 28 for the Mainlanders

## Chao Tung

A teacher of Mandarin (the only officially-designated standard language) at Ilan Middle School, he was the only Mainlander in Ilan to fall victim in the February 28 Incident.

*Chen Chao-chen (student of the deceased):* "It is believed that the death of my teacher may have had to do with the principal, surnamed Li. The principal had been trying to file a lot of false expense reports, but they were all refused by my teacher. There were more than forty students in our class, but not one was absent when the lot of us went to collect the body, for he was very much respected. His suit had been stolen, and his shoes and watch had also disappeared. There were two bullet holes next to his heart. He had been shot from behind, and then kicked into the sea. (From *Kemalan February 28, Independence Evening Post, 1992.*)

## Hsu Cheng

Coming to Taiwan with wife and son to teach university in 1927, after the war Hsu was hired as chief editor of Taiwan's most popular evening paper, the *Ta Ming Pao*. In March, at the age of 39, he was taken from his home, never to be heard from again. Another Mainlander, the paper's publisher and editorial writer Ai Lu-sheng, was also a victim in the February 28 Incident.

*Hsu Chun (son of the deceased):* "Father was arrested on March 15. The next day, Lin Mao-sheng's wife came to our house to ask Father's help in locating her husband. It was then that Mother knew that this was not just a coincidence. Unable to wait, Mother, with four kids in tow, visited the Military Police, the Garrison Command

L13

Hsu Cheng and his wife

and other units in search of them. Later she lost hope, and decided to take us all to the river and commit suicide, but hearing my four-year-old brother say that he wanted to take care of the crab that he had caught, Mother could control her pain no longer, and let out a cry to the heavens. Never since have I seen her in such pain." (From "From Strange Land to Homeland: Mainlander Image Exhibition," *Dove of Peace* No. 14, Taipei 228 Memorial Museum, 2000.)

# Feeble Flame of Justice
## The 1950s & 1960s

**Even though this was the age of silence, there were still calls of conscience. Two flowers that prematurely withered that chill winter were the magazines *Free China* and *Wenhsing*.**

Bringing together Lei Chen, Hu Shih, Yin Hai-kuang, Fu Cheng and other liberal intellectuals, *Free China* offered critiques striking out at the vitals of the dictatorial regime, for which the KMT regarded it as having "poisonous thoughts." For having joined some native-Taiwanese young talents in organizing the anti-KMT China Democratic Party, Lei Chen was sentenced to ten years' imprisonment, and *Free China* was banned.

*Wenhsing (Apollo)* brought such intellectuals as Lee Ao, Yin Hai-kuang, Li Sheng-ting and Lu Hsiao-chao under its banner, and broadly introduced western liberal thought and human rights ideals. With the closing of *Free China*, *Wenhsing* became the formative classic for young students, on whom it had a great influence. In 1965, it too was closed by the KMT.

*Free China* and *Wenhsing* were the bastions of liberalism in the Taiwan of that period, but since they were publications and not organizations, they lacked a mass base and were easily killed off. Yet, despite the treacherous environment, they represented epoch-making calls for democracy and human rights that broke the deadly silence of the times.

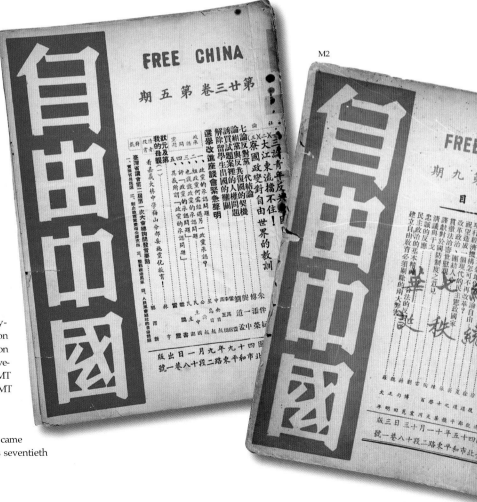

*Left*: *Free China*'s last issue, the "Party-Organizing Special Edition." The opposition party-organizing action of 1960 forged a union of Mainlander intellectual elements and native-Taiwanese people of talent to oppose the KMT dictatorship. The initiative failed when the KMT began arresting.

*Right*: The November 1956 special edition came out on the occasion of Chiang Kai-shek's seventieth birthday.

# Lei Chen (1897~1979)

In 1949 the Chiang Kai-shek regime fled to its Taiwan exile. With the repression of the February 28 Incident, Taiwan came under the White Terror. When Lei Chen started *Free China* in Taipei, that settled his uncommon and tragic fate.

*Free China* was a publication upholding democracy, freedom and anticommunism. At the time of its establishment, its anticommunist character made it the iconic publication of the KMT regime, which was isolated and in need of support. But the outbreak of the Korean War brought an end to the crisis for the Chiang regime, and thereafter the publication's ideas concerning democracy and freedom became a provocation that Chiang Kai-shek found intolerable.

Its 1951 editorial, "The Government Cannot Seduce the People to Crimes," was the first

M3

Lei Chen in front of the magazine offices. He was arrested shortly after. As revealed in official files later made public, Chiang Kai-shek personally ordered that Lei should be sentenced to not less than ten years.

to come under repression by the combined forces of the party, the

government and the military. In 1955, for having investigated the disciplining of party members, Lei Chen, formerly at the power center of the KMT, was expelled from the party.

In 1956, in the name of celebrating Chiang Kai-shek's seventieth birthday, the magazine put out a special edition that lost him much face, for it advocated freedom of speech and nationalization of the military, and criticized his dictatorial rule. From 1957 onwards, it started a comprehensive examination of the political system, and championed the organizing of an opposition party.

In 1960, Lei Chen was arrested, *Free China* banned from publishing, and its leading lights, such as Yin Hai-kuang and Fu Cheng, came under various sorts of sanctions.

# Declaration of Taiwan People's Self-Salvation (1964)

Unlike in the 1950s, Taiwan Independence cases started to take center stage in the 1960s. Among them, the one receiving the most attention was that which advanced a full-blown Taiwan Independence theory—the "Declaration of Taiwan People's Self-Salvation" case in 1964.

The central character in the story was Peng Ming-min (1923~ ), at the time a much-respected professor in the Political Science Department at National Taiwan University. Together with two of his students, Wei Ting-chao and Hsieh Tsung-min (Roger Hsieh), he proposed a "one China, one Taiwan" theory, and had fliers printed up and was preparing to circulate them throughout the island. But before distribution even

M4

*Left to right*: Hsieh Tsung-min, Peng Ming-min and Wei Ting-chao. Wei (1936~1999) was imprisoned three times, serving a total of seventeen years, while Hsieh (1934~ ) went in twice, for a total of twelve years. Peng did 22 years in exile.

got started, they were arrested and given heavy sentences. In 1970, Peng slipped out of Taiwan secretly, and

did not return until 1992, to go on to run for president in 1996.

## Su Tung-chi Case (1961)

A first-generation Taiwan democrat, Su Tung-chi (1923~1992) was elected to the Yunlin County Council four times, and took part in Lei Chen's party-organizing movement. He was arrested in 1961 for his involvement in a plan for armed revolution, and the following year was sentenced to death, but, thanks to a show of support from his fellow-councilors and to international concern, it was changed to life imprisonment. Pictured is Su, *right*, after his release, together with his wife, Su Hung Yueh-chiao, *left*, and human rights activist Oshima Koh'ichi, as they participate in an activity in Japan in support of Shih Ming-teh.

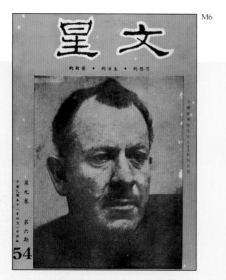

M6

*Wenhsing Magazine (Apollo)* (1957~1965) provided a broad introduction to progressive thought from the West, and was a formative lesson in democracy and human rights. The April 1962 issue's cover personality was the 1962 winner of the Nobel Prize in Literature, John Steinbeck, described by the magazine as "spokesman of the underclass."

This picture shows the extent to which Chiang Kai-shek was lauded as giant and savior of the Republic of China.

M7

## Chiang Kai-shek Deification Movement

Beginning in 1950, Chiang Kai-shek, having lost the support of the people on the mainland, was remolded in Taiwan into the perfect great man. Throughout the island, schools, parks and streets were named after him in profusion. His statues came to occupy every campus, his picture every classroom, while his every word became required reading in the course load. He was modeled into the conveyor of Chinese historical and cultural orthodoxy, a sagacious thinker, and the leader who would save the innumerable suffering masses.

M8

*Free China* group picture. *Fourth from the right in the third row* is Lei Chen, the magazine's founder; *second from the right* is chief editorial writer Yin Hai-kuang; *second from the left in the first row* is editor-in-chief Fu Cheng, and *center in the middle row* is Hu Shih.

## The World and Taiwan in the 1960s

The 1960s were the most bountiful period in modern history. The anti-war movement in the US, the student movements in South Korea and France, the South African black people's anti-apartheid protests, the Prague Spring in Czechoslovakia—all these challenged authority and constraints, while seeking a new idealism and vision. The sparks of human rights were igniting everywhere, but contrasted with this was Taiwan, where under Martial Law all remained quiet, almost as if it had no place on the world map.

## One China: Taiwan's Failed Diplomacy

In the late 1960s, at a time when international society was already putting recognition of China on the diplomatic agenda, Chiang Kai-shek was resolutely holding forth as representative of the China "orthodoxy." In the last few years of his life, taking no heed of the desire of other countries to recognize both China and Taiwan, Chiang insisted on playing a zero-sum game with China on the stage of international diplomacy. And so, should any country wish to establish relations with the People's Republic of China, they would necessarily have to break relations with Taiwan, which absolutely refused to change its name from the "Republic of China."

Chiang had a very deep and far-reaching influence on Taiwan, such that even now Taiwan has no international status, and the vast majority of countries do not recognize as fact that Taiwan is a sovereign and independent country. Taiwan's attempts at returning to international society still meet all sorts of difficulties.

M9

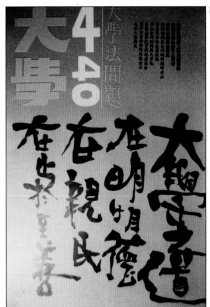

*Tahsueh Magazine (The Intellectual)* was an important political review of the 1960s and 1970s, during which time it proposed that the national legislature be completely reelected.

# The Rising Call for Human Rights

## The 1970s

**Before he died in 1975, Chiang Kai-shek had already prepared the way for his successor, his son Chiang Ching-kuo, who had started his career as head of the secret police. The son's methods exceeded even those of the father, and the facts prove that the age of Chiang Ching-kuo was another peak in Taiwan's dictatorial rule. But at the same time the native opposition (known as the Tangwai) was gathering strength, and the 1970s became the transitional period when opposition to the regime of Chiang Ching-kuo brought lots of frustrations for the Tangwai.**

The history of the Tangwai may be traced back to the 1950s, when there was a very small group of people in the Taiwan Provincial Assembly who called themselves "non-party, non-faction." They included Wu San-lien, Kuo Yu-hsin, and Hsu Shih-hsien. In the 1970s a new generation of native talent rose through the ranks, among them Huang Hsin-chieh, Kang Ning-hsiang and Chang Chun-hung. They ran for office formally as the "Tangwai," thereby taking the lonely fight of the dissident elements to the level of political organization.

For the Tangwai people to take part in elections was very difficult, because the mainstream media, virtually all of which served as nothing more than Kuomintang mouthpiece, would either sling mud and try to destroy their reputations, or gang up on them. As for the KMT, if it was not buying votes then it was rigging the count, resulting in defeat for many of the electoral victors. And even if the Tangwai candidates should get elected, they had their phones tapped, were spied upon, and were split up. When these measures did not suffice, they were thrown in jail.

The Chungli Incident of 1977 was a milestone in the development of the movement for democracy and human rights. This is the first time that the Taiwan masses had spontaneously taken to the streets to protest election irregularities, and was the opening act in a series of street demonstrations. After that, during the 1980s and 1990s, the people at the base of society made their voices heard through marches and demonstrations. With their gain in collective power, they were able to shake the confidence of the dictatorial regime and the Martial Law system, but tremendous sacrifice was still required.

N1

**Background photo: the November 19, 1977 Chungli Incident**
In the 1977 election for county magistrate, an angry crowd gathered to protest KMT ballot rigging. Two young people were shot to death by the police.

"Our Appeal," the second statement by the Presbyterian Church in Taiwan, November 18, 1975.

"A Declaration on Human Rights," the third statement by Presbyterian Church in Taiwan , August 16, 1977.

# The Presbyterians' Three Declarations (1971~1977)

Taiwan's political situation was pretty bleak in the 1970s as the crisis deepened. On the foreign affairs front there were serious setbacks, while domestically, busy with its deification of Chiang Kai-shek and Chiang Ching-kuo, the regime was stamping out all opposition. Therefore, the issuing of three declarations by the Presbyterian Church in Taiwan was all the more stunning.

The PCT, which began proselytizing in Taiwan in 1865, established the first Western-style school and the first newspaper, and prepared both the first publicly-funded student for study abroad and the first person to go on to earn a Ph.D. Since putting down roots more than one hundred years ago, its heart has been beating as one with Taiwan society.

In 1971, as Taiwan left the United Nations and set about busily breaking relations with many countries, it became an international orphan. It was then that the PCT issued its first statement calling for respect of Taiwan's human rights, proposing a complete reelection of the national legislature and self-determination for the people of Taiwan.

In 1975, the KMT banned Bibles that had been translated into native Taiwanese. The PCT issued a second statement, calling for freedom of religion and social justice.

In 1977, as the United States was about to establish relations with the PRC and end military aid to Taiwan, the PCT issued its third statement, proposing that "Taiwan should become a new and independent country."

All three of these statements were as far-sighted as they were epoch-making. Coming at a time when the Tangwai movement had yet to reach maturity, these calls for democracy and human rights communicated directly from Taiwan to an international audience were of tremendous encouragement to Taiwan society. But afterwards, the secretary-general of the Church's general assembly, Reverend Kao Chun-ming, was arrested in 1980 and sentenced to seven years.

Nevertheless, history has proven that Taiwan's course of reform has, step by step, realized the proposals put forth in the three statements. After they were issued, the Tangwai began to coalesce as an island-wide force. Add to all of this the baptism of fire of the Chungli Incident, and the movement for democracy and human rights leaped forward to a new stage.

### Early Tangwai

Democrats of the preceding generation began their careers through popular elections. *From left*, the "five dragons and a phoenix" were: Li Wan-chu, Kuo Yu-hsin, Hsu Shih-hsien, Kuo Kuo-chi, Wu San-lien, and Li Yuan-chan.

### Wu San-lien (1899~1988)

*Standing, second from right*, from Tainan, Wu San-lien served as Taipei mayor, and headed the *Independence Evening Post* in his struggle for freedom of the press. His son, Wu Yi-min, spent thirteen years in prison for having participated in a left-wing reading club.

### Kuo Kuo-chi (1900~1970)

From Kaohsiung, Kuo served terms in both the Taiwan Provincial Assembly and the Legislative Yuan, and was known as "Big Gun Kuo."

N7

### Hsu Shih-hsien (1908~1983)

Mayor of Chiayi City, Hsu originally hailed from Tainan and was known as the "Matsu from Chiayi"—Matsu being Taiwan's most-beloved goddess.

N8

### Li Wan-chu (1902~1966)

From Yunlin, Li was the founder of the newspaper *Public Forum*, and fought for freedom of speech.

N9

### Kuo Yu-hsin (1908~1985)

In the Taiwan Provincial Assembly for 21 years, Kuo was the leader of the Ilan opposition, which had a long and proud heritage, not to mention a tremendous influence on both the Tangwai and the Democratic Progressive Party.

N10

### Human Rights Logo

Chang Fu-chung designed this spiritual emblem of the Tangwai in 1978. It conveyed the will to struggle, and was called the "black fist" by the right wing.

N11

N12

### Overseas Concern for Taiwan Human Rights

The Taiwan Political Prisoner Rescue Association in Japan showed its concern over the repression of human rights by the Taiwan authorities by initiating a popular movement appealing for human rights in Taiwan.

N13

## Tangwai Political Rallies

In the later Tangwai period every election featured government-sanctioned "political rallies" in which the candidates would present their views to the public. Turnout typically numbered in the tens of thousands, yet by the time of the count the ballots of the Tangwai supporters—no surprise—had been "eliminated" through various Kuomintang tricks.

N14

## Taiwan Political Review (August~December 1975)

This was an important political publication led by Huang Hsin-chieh, Kang Ning-hsiang and Chang Chun-hung. It lasted all of five issues before being banned by the KMT.

## Tangwai "National Affairs Statement"

On the eve of the severing of US-ROC relations in 1979, the Tangwai issued a statement advocating that the fate of Taiwan be decided by the Taiwanese people themselves. Shown here are the signers, with Huang Shun-hsing, *left*, and Yu Teng-fa, *right*. Chen Chu and Shih Ming-teh are standing first and second from the right. Yu was magistrate of Kaohsiung County at the time. In 1989 he was assassinated under circumstances that are unclear to this day.

# The Kaohsiung Incident
## 1979 and the Early 1980s

**On International Human Rights Day in 1979, the Kaohsiung Incident broke out, with a force that had far-reaching impact. This was to have been a march commemorating human rights, but conflict was brewing once they had been surrounded by MPs and police. Afterwards the KMT carried out island-wide mass arrests, and the Tangwai Group, which had been built over the previous decade through so much toil and struggle, was nearly wiped out.**

In the military court trials which followed, the Tangwai leadership was charged with "rebellion" and given sentences ranging from over ten years in prison to life. During the trials, the mother and twin daughters of one of the defendants, Lin Yi-hsiung, were killed in a bloody incident. In 1981, Dr. Chen Wen-chen, PhD, a mathematician teaching in the US, returned to Taiwan and was called in by the Garrison Command for interrogation. His body was discovered on the campus of National Taiwan University. In 1985, Wu Shu-jen, wife of one of the Kaohsiung Incident defense lawyers, Chen Shui-bian, was seriously injured in a suspicious truck accident. From these three incidents can be seen the bitter trials suffered by the democratic movement for human rights.

The Kaohsiung Incident was the great wake-up call for the movement. The appeal to human rights by the defendants and their political criticism prompted a response from the public, around which a new force for reform could coalesce. The facts prove that this was a very important turning point in modern Taiwan history, a milestone on the Taiwan people's road toward directing their own destiny.

O1

**Formosa Group Kaohsiung March**
Once the marching public had been tightly surrounded, tensions were heightened considerably, leading to the outbreak of violence.

O2

**Formosa Monthly**

Established in 1979, the *Formosa Monthly*'s premier issue sold over 100,000 copies, breaking all records for a Taiwan magazine. The publishing group established branch offices and service centers throughout the island, and began to take on the shape of a political party.

### Rescue Work

This four-page bulletin published in Japan by the Taiwan Political Prisoner Rescue Association covered the Kaohsiung Incident, the Lin Yi-hsiung family murders, and the Watarida Masahiro case*, all of which were important cases of political repression in 1979 and 1980. Rescue work by overseas human rights organizations meant that the KMT felt even greater international pressure when repressing dissidents.

*Leaving Taiwan on December 21, 1979, Watarida, a Japanese tourist, was arrested at the airport when he was caught carrying materials on the Kaohsiung Incident suspects and Taiwan Independence activists. The authorities sentenced him to three years' reform education, but the sentence was not carried out, and instead he was expelled.*

04

The Lin residence, where the killings took place, was converted to a church sanctuary, the Gikong Church, whose name symbolizes the broadcasting of hope in a land of hardship.

05

## Woodblock Print of the Lin Twins

The killing of Lin Yi-hsiung's family members was a political plot. From this print commemorating the taking of two innocent girls can be seen the dangers of political activity at the time and the ordeals undergone by the democratic movement. It is testimony to the great pain felt in Taiwanese hearts.

06

## Dr. Chen Wen-chen and Family

This happy family experienced tragic upheaval on July 2, 1981. Chen's murder remains unsolved. It is generally regarded as the work of political assassins.

07

## Gloomy Parade

After the murder of Chen Wen-chen, overseas Taiwanese organized demonstrations. From the marchers, here wearing masks to hide their identity from KMT spies, we can see at a glance the climate of fear that hung over the heads of those who dared to express their conscience—even abroad.

**City/Area** POST-GAZETTE: Mon., July 20, 1981 — 3

# vill probe Chen's death, legislator promises

Demonstrators march in Oakland on Saturday to protest the mysterious death in Taiwan of Dr. Wen-chen Chen.

Paul Siantis/Post-Gazette

support of the ruling Taiwanese government and dispute allegations that Chen, a native of Taipei, was murdered for his political views.

Several speakers bowed in the direction of a large floral wreath bearing Chen's picture.

A dozen speakers extolled the 31-year-old professor who was found July 3 on the library at National University in Taipei. To the Association for Chen traveled a long who hard to advance sought a taste of session that always pressed in his

Nieckarr of the Ossining, N.Y., name in Taiwan and one who eves victory. with you in this

moment of pain and tragedy," he said. "Professor Chen was a scholar and patriot who joins the brotherhood of all those who would rather die than be imprisoned by deceit and injustice."

Hsu-Steve of New York expressed gratitude for support given Chen's family by Richard Cyert, CMU president, and by Chen's colleagues. Morris DeGroot, an associate in the Statistics Department, described Chen as a leading researcher in the field of statistics and probabilities, "a brilliant young scientist." Stephen Fienberg, chairman of the CMU Statistics Department, said a seminar to be held at CMU in October will be dedicated in Chen's honor.

Other speakers, some of whom did not identify themselves, praised Chen for courage in speaking out against injustice and dictatorship, as a man with a strong sense of social justice, a supporter of human

rights. Some spoke in Taiwanese, their voices breaking, eyes filled with tears.

Then the group, many carrying banners, marched through Oakland to the Pitt campus, with a police escort. Chanting "KMT murdered Dr. Chen," "Justice to Dr. Chen," "Taiwan for Taiwanese," "KMT spies out of campus," and other slogans, the group wound its way back to Hunt Library, where the memorial service had been held.

Two minor incidents took place during the afternoon. Before the service began, a student believed to be a Kuomintang sympathizer took pictures of some participants. He was asked to leave.

During the march, at Forbes Avenue and Bigelow Boulevard, an Asian watching the demonstration was chased and shouted at by several marchers who felt he was a progovernment sympathizer trying to keep a record of the marchers. But

when he spoke in Mandarin, official language of the Chinese mainland, they said he was not a Taiwanese and gave up the chase.

In Los Angeles, the American wife of a Taiwanese dissident was arrested Saturday on charges she splattered red paint at the Taiwan visa office in protest of Chen's death.

Linda Arrigo, 32, of San Diego was arrested while a protest was going on outside the visa office by persons concerned with a crackdown on political dissent by the Taiwan government.

Arrigo is married to Shi Mingdeh, 38, who recently was sentenced to life in prison in Taiwan for sedition. She was deported from Taiwan in 1979 for anti-government activities.

About 70 persons demonstrated in Los Angeles against the Taiwan government to protest Chen's death.

08

## Fatal Contribution Receipt

With the establishment of *Formosa Monthly*, overseas Taiwanese rushed to contribute. Making no effort to hide the fact, Chen Wen-chen had signed this contribution receipt, which led the Garrison Command to call him in for questioning, after which he was never seen alive again.

09

### The Road of Love and Politics

Chen Shui-bian (pushing the wheelchair) was one of the defending lawyers in the Kaohsiung Incident case, and later became a shining star on the political scene. Here he is seen with his wife Wu Shu-jen in the streets soliciting votes for the north Taipei electoral district seat in the 1989 legislative election. After becoming first lady in 2000, Wu worked to expand Taiwan's international diplomatic space.

# Blacklist Stories

"Pining for my homeland, with its beautiful mountains and rivers, still thousands of miles away...." The song "Missing Home" was written in the 1950s by a victim of the White Terror. Together with the song "Homeland Sunset," it became an elegy to homesickness that the overseas Taiwanese sang in the 1970s and 1980s. Not only had they put their homeland thousands of miles behind them, but, thanks to the blacklist, these Taiwanese were now stuck abroad for decades.

The Taiwan of martial law was a country sealed off from the outside. On the one hand, people were restricted from touring abroad, while on the other the country was excluded from the world stage. The blacklist policy adopted a two-track course—both banning people the KMT did not like from entering, and barring those it did not like from leaving the country. The former were primarily overseas students and scholars, while the latter included former political prisoners and dissidents. Most of them represented the most outstanding talent that Taiwan had to offer.

The concocting of the blacklist was owing to the efforts of the secret police and "professional students" whom the KMT had dispatched overseas. They would perform surveillance and file reports on every word and deed, and were the Kuomintang's best informants. Those included on the blacklist were not only prevented from coming back to serve their country after finishing their studies, but couldn't even come back to attend the funeral of a loved one.

There are disparate accounts as to the number blacklisted. At the very least there were hundreds. When Lee Teng-hui came to power in 1988 and his power had yet to be firmly established, the military strongman Hau Pei-tsun supported the blacklist policy, so that the only way overseas Taiwanese could gain entry was to "crash the gates." Those succeeding were arrested, while those who failed were expelled. In 1992 Lee rescinded the order that had barred some 277 people from returning. These Taiwanese who were exiled and had been pining for their homeland day and night were finally allowed to come back.

The blacklist reflected the KMT mindset at the time, which thought it appropriate to include overseas activities of the Taiwanese within the scope of KMT control and to make overseas activities liable for punishment. This could be likened to PRC interference abroad: when it threatens others for having relations with Taiwan, it both broadened the scope of political repression and interfered with the domestic politics of other countries. Through these blacklisting measures we can begin to appreciate the breadth and complexity of Taiwan's human rights problems.

# We Want Human Rights!
## The Late 1980s

### 1986, Storm of Controversy

Big changes started to come in the late 1980s, especially in 1986 and 1987, the two crucial years in which social forces broke free and in which democratic and human rights developments accelerated. The two events with the most far-reaching influence were the establishment of the Democratic Progressive Party and the rescinding of martial law.

The establishment of the DPP had a close connection with the Kaohsiung Incident, after which Tangwai publications found a larger audience and broke through the taboos on public expression. The defending lawyers and families of the Kaohsiung Incident defendants, embracing the will to sacrifice, established the DPP on September 28, 1986. Up until this time, the ban on opposition parties had been strenuously enforced, with the KMT's policy of "no party outside the party, no faction within the party" making for a total monopoly on national resources for over four decades.

The May 19 Green Action launched by Cheng Nan-jung appealed for an end to martial law, opening a series of street demonstrations that lasted for half a year. Another wave of opposition came from the environmental movement, with the people of Lukang opposing the locating of a Dupont factory in their neighborhood and awakening people to a new concern for sustainable development.

1986 was the social movement's time of upheaval, with countless demonstrations confronting the barricades, riot control police and other trappings of the martial law system. This was also the age of Taiwan's great economic take-off, when within three years the stock market had raced from one thousand points to ten thousand. Millionaires proliferated, allowing people the extra time to take up social reform and pursue a life of dignity.

P1

民主新希望
新黨救台灣

### 在運動中一起成長

民主進步黨是誕生於寬闊的街頭與人民的懷抱，而不是誕生於僵化的議會與統治者的樊籠；民主進步黨是成長於街頭的露滋與人民的照護，而不是成長於議會的點滴與統治者的飼養；街頭的所在與人民的所在，也就是民主進步黨生命的依歸與成長的所在

> 民主進步黨是一個屬於全體人民，爲人民爭取、保障基本人權的政黨。

如果您已年滿十八歲，認同民進黨的綱領，志願服膺民進黨黨章之規定，願意加入民進黨的話，請您向花蓮縣民主進步促進會索取入黨申請表。

如果您還沒有決定要加入，但想要了解民進黨的黨綱和黨章，歡迎您向本會索取有關資料。

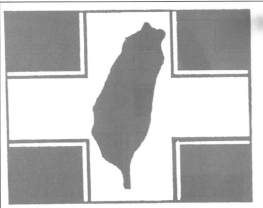

民主進步黨　組黨說明會

江鵬堅・謝長廷・尤　清・周清玉
顏錦福・邱義仁・吳乃仁・許國泰
黃煌雄・朱高正・游錫堃・貝馨儀

主辦／花蓮縣民主進步促進會
時間／七十六年五月卅日下午七時
地點／花蓮市國風國民中學體育館

民進黨在爲民眾爭取什麼？
民進黨在爲民眾爭取什麼？

花蓮縣民主進步促進會　製作
地址：花蓮市菁華街14號・電話：324188

FREE ALL POLITICAL PRISONERS

釋放所有政治犯

P1: Children from Kungliao in Taipei County hold a placard reading "Fight Nuclear Power Plant Number Four." The nuclear power plant, now under construction, is very close to the metropolis of Taipei, raising safety concerns.

P2&P5: Front and back of a flier announcing the organizing of the Democratic Progressive Party. The above emphasizes that "the DPP is a political party struggling on behalf of the people for basic human rights guarantees," while below is shown the party flag, representing the fact that Taiwan now stands at a historic crossroads, meaning that today Taiwan must become a nation of love and peace.

P3: Scene several days after the founding of the DPP. At right is a portrait of Sun Yat-sen, father of the Chinese republic. The democratic politics that he championed did not see the light of day until 61 years later.

P4: This is a 1985 poster produced by the Taiwan Association for Human Rights, founded the year before, calling for the release of all political prisoners.

P6: University students go to the Legislative Yuan to petition for university autonomy, academic freedom, and the expulsion of military instructors from the campuses.

P7: The Tao people of Orchid Island take action to save their homeland by protesting the Taiwan authorities' siting of a nuclear waste storage facility on their island.

P8: In a demonstration in front of the Presidential Building, people from the historic town of Lukang protest the government's ignoring of the popular will by planning to allow Dupont to site a factory in their area. As a newly developing third world country, Taiwan had had enough of industrial pollution caused by the multinationals.

P6

P7

P8

P9

In 1980 the KMT built the Chiang Kai-shek Memorial Hall to commemorate the dictator. It became the stage for many large-scale demonstrations in the late 1980s, proving the victory of people's power.

# 1987, End of Martial Law

Riding the tidal swell of the 1986 movement for democracy and human rights, the Taiwan of 1987 had a renaissance-like vitality. The February 28 Peace Promotion Association toured Taiwan with various activities, breaking the most sensitive of taboos by expressing the hope that the bloody February 28 Incident would be commemorated as an anniversary of peace and justice. That year, the women, student, Indigenous and consumer movements were all marching forward.

In response to the thundering blows of people's power, the KMT finally rescinded martial law, the world's longest-standing. This monster had imprisoned Taiwan, leaving wounds that would fester long into the future, from every corner of society to the deepest recesses of the individual heart. The most conspicuous of these divisions over ethnic background and national identity have induced social instability. More than this, Taiwan squandered several decades of

P10

The KMT, while announcing the end of martial law and declaring that we were still in a period of "mobilization against the rebellion," established the National Security Law to replace martial law. This roused the people to protest, with demands for "100 percent abrogation of martial law."

opportunities to learn democracy, so that the national legislature has lost its normal function, descending into ugly political fights, and rendering Taiwan's democratic politics a scene of chaos.

P11

P12

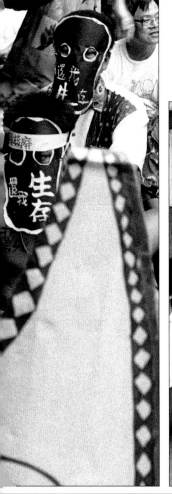

P11: The Tao people of Orchid Island dress up as "radioactive people" to protest the locating on their island of a nuclear waste dump, a threat to their survival. As this book goes to press, the nuclear waste has yet to be removed from an island famed for its butterfly orchids and unique natural scenery.

P12: This march, protesting child prostitution and white slavery, shows that serious women's rights issues still exist in Taiwan.

P13: Anti-nuclear activist Lin Yi-hsiung, *center*, leads a protest against the Kuomintang's decision to build the controversial fourth nuclear power plant without consulting popular opinion. This hunger strike in front of the Legislative Yuan called for a popular referendum on the issue.

P14: Democratic activists stage a silent sit-down strike to fight for freedom of association. At the time, a private organization need only try to register using "Taiwan" in its name to have the application rejected.

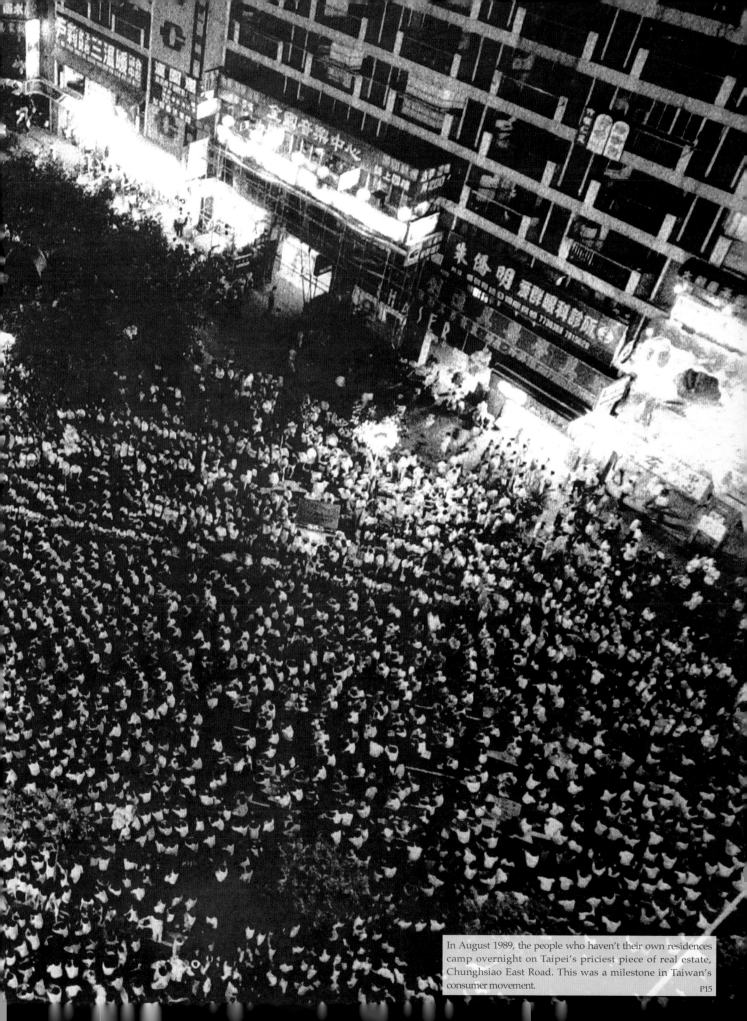

In August 1989, the people who haven't their own residences camp overnight on Taipei's priciest piece of real estate, Chunghsiao East Road. This was a milestone in Taiwan's consumer movement.

P16

In 1987 Chiang Ching-kuo decreed the release of 26 political prisoners, and reduced sentences for 55 more. On this "Human Rights Night," the public enthusiastically welcome home the newly released political prisoners.

P17

P18

The May 20, 1989 demonstration of farmers was the largest protest and suppression since the ending of martial law. That night these farmers and supportive students were beaten by stick-wielding MPs and police. Over seventy people were arrested and sentenced.

One of Taiwan's four main ethnic groups, Hakka people carry a portrait of Sun Yat-sen, himself a Hakka, wearing a face mask. They are protesting the government's long-term suppression of the Hakka language. It was not until 2003 that Taiwan had its first TV station broadcasting in Hakka.

# Cheng Nan-jung (1947~1989)

P19

On April 7, 1989, Cheng Nan-jung brought his illustrious life to a close by setting himself afire in the editorial office of his magazine, *Freedom Era*. His death ignited a tremendous force for the political reform that was to follow.

Under Article 100 of the Criminal Code, the KMT had charged Cheng with "rebellion" for having printed a "Draft for a New Taiwan Constitution" in his magazine. When the KMT made clear its intention to arrest him, Cheng declared, "The KMT cannot arrest my person, just my corpse." With such a determination to die, he protected his ideals: one hundred percent freedom of expression.

At a critical turning point in modern Taiwan history, Cheng Nan-jung did a number of things that had far-reaching influence, including the founding of his *Freedom Era* magazine and fight for freedom of speech, and the founding of the February 28 Peace Promotion Association to seek restitution for Taiwan's worst postwar tragedy. He also supported and organized many marches for Tsai You-chuan and Hsu Tsao-teh, who had been charged with rebellion for advocating Taiwan Independence, and twice applied pressure on the authorities to end martial law with the May 19 Green Action.

All of these activities directly challenged the greatest of the KMT authorities' taboos. By putting his life on the line, Cheng Nan-jung extended protection of democracy and human rights, and forced an end to the siege. He said, "If I press the attack in front, those behind will be able to walk that much more easily." This courageous martyr moved even more people to join the ranks of those opposing injustice.

1986 saw the arrest of the Kuomintang's headache, Cheng Nan-jung. This, his first and only imprisonment, lasted for eight months. Here he is seen arriving handcuffed in court.

P20

The 1987 arrest of two former political prisoners, Tsai You-chuan and Hsu Tsao-teh, for advocating Taiwan independence, brought on an island-wide rescue movement, and pushed the calls for Taiwan Independence to unprecedented heights.

# Taiwan Stands Up
## Human Rights Spring, 1990s

### Reversing the Verdicts, Seeking Release

Taiwanese by the tens of thousands were killed in the February 28 Incident of 1947, following which the White Terror claimed innumerable political prisoners. Forty years later, Cheng Nan-jung, who was born in the year of the February 28 Incident, promoted an island-wide movement, speaking at street protests, marching, and calling for the reversal of the February 28 verdicts and for the release of political prisoners, all in the face of overwhelming riot police forces.

This was the human rights movement that had continued so long and penetrated so deeply. Such demands as justice for the wrongly accused, release of prisoners, apologies, compensation, public revelation of the truth, establishment of memorials, and setting of an anniversary have all been met one by one. By contrast, however, investigation of the basic facts of the White Terror has met with a myriad difficulties.

Whether the February 28 Incident or the White Terror, Taiwan has felt their far-reaching influence. The healing and reconstruction of the collective spirit of the Taiwanese still needs continued effort. Only when Taiwan is allowed to become a country with ongoing guarantees for human rights will the numberless souls who shouted themselves hoarse crying for human rights in those dark years be comforted.

In 1995 the 228 Memorial in Taipei City's 228 Peace Park became reality. As president, Lee Teng-hui offers the first official apology for the violence of the government in 1947. But the violators, whether individual or political party, have until today failed to take any responsibility whatever for the events of either February 28 or the White Terror.

Q1

Q2

➡ To recognize Cheng Nan-jung's great contribution to Taiwan, tens of thousands attend a huge funeral service for him on May 19, 1989. *Second from the right in the front row* is his wife, Yeh Chulan, who later goes on to become legislator and vice premier.

◀ In 1991 several hundred former political prisoners hold a large-scale demonstration calling for the scrapping of Article 100 of the Criminal Code, responsible for wrongful imprisonments beyond number.

Q3

Q4

⬆ In 1993 Legislator Lin Cheng-chieh, *third from left,* and some former political prisoners hold a press conference to publicly announce that the graves of White Terror victims have been discovered at Liuchangli in Taipei.

Q5

◀ Photos of some of the February 28 victims, taken at a public ceremony on behalf of these departed souls.

Q6

➡ In 1996, Lee Teng-hui is elected president, garnering 54% of the vote.

# Lee Teng-hui (1923~ )

The first native-Taiwanese president, Lee Teng-hui's twelve years in office stretched from 1988 to 2000. During that time Taiwan went from martial law to democracy, its closed society became an open one, and the KMT gradually transformed from foreign regime to native. All of these changes were mainly because the "great China" designs for Taiwan were relaxed, and the island's centrality was established. To protect Taiwan's sovereignty, Lee proposed the "two-state theory" for Taiwan and China, rebuking the two parties—the KMT and the CCP—for having China in their names, and for giving extended support to the "one-China" policy.

His surpassing achievement won for him the name "Mr. Democracy," and he is today regarded as helmsman of Taiwan's "peaceful revolution." His contributions for democracy and human rights have encouraged others to throw themselves into reform, and to strive for a beautiful Taiwanese future.

Q7

Q8

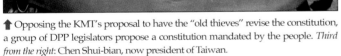

⬆ Calling them "old thieves," a huge crowd in front of the Chiang Kai-shek Memorial Hall demands that the "10,000-year people's representatives" step down.

⬆ Opposing the KMT's proposal to have the "old thieves" revise the constitution, a group of DPP legislators propose a constitution mandated by the people. *Third from the right*: Chen Shui-bian, now president of Taiwan.

Q10

Q11

Q9

➡ Presidential election under the gun: in 1996 the election was held under the threat of missiles from China. Lee Teng-hui took up campaign activities with the armed protection of security personnel.

Q12

⬆ ⬅ *Above and left*: The people's lifetime representatives, not subject to reelection, were once world-class laughing stock but have now become history.

# The Peaceful Revolution

When Chiang Ching-kuo died in January 1988, the KMT's Taiwan-born Lee Teng-hui rose to power and began the painful process of political reform. The confluence of three forces—Lee Teng-hui, the DPP and mainstream popular opinion—took on the challenge of Taiwan's "three disasters."

The first of these took the form of the old representatives in the National Assembly, who declared themselves representatives of the Chinese "orthodoxy," and who had not stood for election in forty years. The second was the system whereby the president was elected by old National Assembly members without so much as a trace of popular support. And the third was the ruling party, which controlled all the national resources, and could not be removed no matter the extent of its corruption.

So as to bring these oddities to an end, Taiwan developed its thorny "peaceful revolution." First, in 1991 and 1992, the entire national legislature stood for reelection. Then, in 1996, the president was directly elected by the people. Finally, with the presidential election of 2000, Taiwan saw its first peaceful transfer of power.

These three great projects were accomplished without bloodshed, despite formidable opposition. Fortunately, with the vast popular will forming a central current, reform—the fruit of the previous twenty years' mighty movement for democracy and human rights—became possible.

Q13

On April 19, 1992 a great street march initiated by the DPP for direct election of the president faces down riot police.

# March 1990 Student Movement

By February 1990 calls for political reform had already reached a thunderous tide of anger. But the conservative faction of the KMT was prepared to conspire with the representatives of the National Assembly, scorned as a bunch of "old thieves." Their aim was to use the opportunity of the old thieves' election of the president to usurp Lee Teng-hui's power while expanding their own. Lee, then vice president, took the seat of Chiang Ching-kuo after his death, with power relations yet to stabilize.

The plan to steal Lee's power and increase their own provoked the antipathy of the masses, and led thousands of university students to do a sit-down in front of the Chiang Kai-shek Memorial Hall. Called the "March Student Movement," it was the largest student demonstration of the post-war era, and it forced the conservative wing of the KMT to take stock and retreat. Winning the presidency, Lee promised the

Q14

Chiang Ching-kuo and his man Hau Pei-tsun, *left*

students that he would call together representatives from the ruling party and the opposition for a "National Affairs Conference." The NAC came out with some very important conclusions, including that of ending the period of civil war, the putting of all seats in the Legislative Yuan up for election, direct election of the provincial governor, and popular election of the president. All of these had far-reaching consequences for the political situation.

The NAC helped Lee Teng-hui secure popular support and push through reforms. Yet the power of the conservative faction was still enough to force him to nominate military strongman Hau Pei-tsun to the post of premier. In May 1990 students and activists again demonstrated against military rule, marking yet another high tide of student protest. But Hau still held on to his job for close to three years, until Lee Teng-hui's power base had stabilized, at which time Hau was replaced.

# Abolition of Bad Laws (1991~1992)

One of the main curses of the White Terror repression was a set of bad laws that included the Statutes for the Punishment of Rebellion, and the Article 100 of the Criminal Code, which specified the "crime of preparing for or plotting domestic rebellion," all of which continued to exist after the 1987 rescinding of martial law.

In 1991 the Bureau of Investigation arrested on charges of "preparing for rebellion" four young intellectuals, including Chen Cheng-jan, involved in a Taiwan Independence organization led by Su Beng. This provoked society to indignation at what was regarded as a serious violation of human rights. Students, professors and cultural organizations formed an Alliance to Oppose Political Repression that pushed to scrap the bad laws, ultimately forcing the Legislative Yuan to abolish the Statutes for the Punishment of Rebellion that May.

In September 1991 the respected scholars Li Chen-yuan, Lin Shan-tien, Chang Chung-tung and Chen Shih-meng brought social movement organizations together to form the Action 100 Alliance to raise a cry to abolish Article 100 of the Criminal Code. They continued to demonstrate, forcing the Legislative Yuan to revise the law in 1992, and to do away with the article specifying the "crime of preparing for or plotting domestic rebellion." This was a great breakthrough for the human rights movement.

In August 1992, the Taiwan Garrison Command, which had long played the role of "assassin of human rights," was scrapped, along with various agencies, such as the Second Personnel Section, which were responsible for overseeing and controlling thought. The Taiwanese people, with ever more confidence, could now wave goodbye to the shadow of the White Terror.

Q15

Academia Sinica scholar Li Chen-yuan, *front row, third from the left,* legal scholar Prof. Lin Shan-tien, *front row, third from the right,* and economist Prof. Chen Shih-meng, *front row, second from the left,* were for abolishing the bad laws. Here they are seen putting their studies aside to participate in a street demonstration.

## Come Home, Child

Every day at dusk, mothers and fathers stand in silence at the door, looking down the road. Their children disappeared years ago, during 228 or the White Terror. There will be no return. Yet every evening their fathers and mothers stand in silence at the door, in the deepening dusk.

Painted by Auyang Wen

## On the Front Lines Abroad
# Secrets of the Overseas Rescue Network

**Starting in the 1960s, overseas efforts to rescue Taiwan's political prisoners were spawned over several decades, with countless individuals and groups participating in this noble endeavor— a humanitarian cause demanding perseverance.**

**This chapter covers six major areas of the overseas rescue network: overseas Taiwanese, church groups, foreign friends, Amnesty International, media and press, and official organizations and academia. Materials have been provided by the Wu San-lien Taiwan Historical Materials Foundation and are taken from their Lynn Miles Collection.**

## Urgent Action—Rescue Transcending National Borders

The overseas effort to rescue Taiwan's political prisoners began in the 1960s. In 1961, the Taiwan Independence Alliance in Japan launched a campaign for Su Tung-chi's case, and sent petition letters to representatives in the US Congress. The overseas Taiwanese and international human rights groups also took action to support the 1964 "Declaration of Taiwan People's Self-Salvation." However, these were only isolated events that generated some rescue effort.

It was at the end of the 1960s that the international human rights movement began to develop rapidly. The Taiwan political prisoner overseas rescue network became more organized, systematic and diversified. In the mid-1970s, the human rights diplomacy of US President Jimmy Carter brought human rights issues to the forefront of international politics, in the course of which the KMT's notorious human rights record of oppression came into the world spotlight and generated considerable international concern.

In 1970, Tsai Tsai-yuan and other political prisoners at the Martial Law Section Jail handed a list of 237 political prisoners to Tsai Mao-tang, who had already left prison. Tsai gave the list to Michael Thornberry, an American pastor teaching at the Taiwan Theological

College and Seminary. Thornberry had it delivered to writer Meng Hsiang-ke, from whom it went to Lee Ao, who in turn handed it to Hsieh Tsung-min, who contacted the secretary general of Amnesty International, Martin Ennals. The story of Taiwan's political prisoners had finally come to the attention of the international community, arousing concern and attracting assistance.

In the 1980s, the KMT took advantage of the momentum at the Kaohsiung Incident and began arresting opposition activists on a massive scale. Such actions provoked anger and brought on a strong reaction from the world community. Under tremendous international pressure, the KMT had to be more cautious and discrete in its oppressive measures against the human rights movement in Taiwan. This was a milestone in the rescue of Taiwan's political prisoners: open international humanitarian rescue efforts, combined with Taiwan's own struggle for human rights, made it possible to see the light at the end of the tunnel—ultimately ending the tragedy of political imprisonment in Taiwan.

## LIST OF TAIWAN POLITICAL PRISONERS (CA. DEC. 1970)

Legend to the list appears at bottom of list. Where asterik appears in any entry, please consult that number under respective column heading

| | NAME | PROV-INCE | AGE | OCCUPATION | DATE AND AGENCY OF ARREST | | CHARGE | ACTUAL OFFENSE |
|---|---|---|---|---|---|---|---|---|
| 1. | Yang Tzu-chieh | D | 42 | Retired military personnel | | | 2/3 | Criticized the Kuomintang |
| 2. | Juan Kuei-yao | D | 43 | | | | 5 | On mainland took part in Erh-t'ung T'uan |
| 3. | Ch'iao Heng-wei | D | 54 | Menial, Legislative Yüan | | | 5 | Escaped from communist-held territory |
| 4. | Li Ta-en | B | 56 | Chief, Tainan tax office | | | 5 | Escaped from communist-held territory |
| 5. | Wang Yü-an | F | 38 | Publisher, Cheng Yen Publishing Co. | CFC | 69.6.30 | 7 | Published left-wing books |
| 6. | Shen Ch'iu-ho | F | 48 | Proprietor, Pai Ch'eng Book Store | | | 7 | Published left-wing books |
| 7. | Ch'iu Yen-liang | E | 35 | Student, NTU* Dept of Archeology | SS | 1968.6 | 2/3 | Marxist study group |
| 8. | Wang Chia-fah | A | 40 | | | 1954 | 7 | |
| 9. | Chang Yüan-lung | D | 46 | Restaurant proprietor | FBI | 62.7.16 | 2/1 | On mainland took part [Red] organization |
| 10. | Fan Ken-ts'ai | C | 48 | Taiwan bank | | | 2/1 | |
| 11. | Hua Ch'un-lin | D | — | Retired military personnel | FBI | 68.5.7 | 2/3 | Criticized the Kuomintang |
| 12. | Ch'en Ch'i-mao | — | — | Trading house | | | 2/1 | On mainland took part [Red] organization |
| 13. | Wang Che-hsing | H | J | — | FBI | 1961 | 2/3 | Implicated by friend(s) |
| 14. | Chang P'ei-hung | D | I | Colonel, regimental vice-commander | | | 5 | Escaped from communist-held territory |
| 15. | Sun Yu-p'u | D | — | Police officer | PD | 1965 | 5 | On mainland took part [Red] organization |
| 16. | Chou Hsia | I | — | Retired captain | FBI | 1960 | 2/3 | Discontented with status quo |
| 17. | Chou Li-chün | A | — | Sec'y, Materials Sect, KMT Cent. Com. | | | 5 | Escaped from communist-held territory |
| 18. | Lin Hsin-chao | — | — | | | | 5 | Plotted Taiwan Independence |
| 19. | Ching Kuo-shu | M | — | Reporter | | | 2/3 | Criticized the Kuomintang |
| 20. | Ho Pi | L | — | Special Commissioner, Chin Ting | | | 2/1 | |
| 21. | T'ang Hsi-ling | C | 54 | | FBI | 1969.4 | 5 | Listened to mainland broadcasts |
| 22. | Cheng T'ien-yü | B | 54 | Sec'y, Keelung Municipal Assembly | FBI | 1968.9 | 2/3 | Had once joined CP (1945) |
| 23. | Ch'i Jung-pao | — | — | Student | | | 7 | |
| 24. | Hung Ch'ing-po | — | B | Farmer from the mainland | | | 2/3 | Discontented with status quo |
| 25. | Su Yung-nien | E | 51 | Retired captain & education officer | FBI | 1961 | 2/1 | Taken captive and brought back |
| 26. | Hsü Mo-kuang | B | — | Deckhand from Hong Kong | | | 2/1 | Took part Hong Kong leftwing labor union |
| 27. | Chang Wei-kuang | C | — | Police officer | | | 7 | |
| 28. | Lin Feng | A | — | Teacher (Chin Ting) | | | 5 | |
| 29. | Ch'i Sheng-kang | H | 20 | Student (Huwei High School) | | | 7 | Listened to [mainland] broadcasts |
| 30. | Lo Chen-hsiang | E | — | Craftsman of rattan ware | FBI | | 2/3 | Took part Red labor union |
| 31. | Ch'en K'un-Shan | A | 32 | Accountant | PD | | 7 | Plotted Taiwan Independence |
| 32. | Liu Chin-shih | A | 37 | Tanner | PD | | 5 | Plotted Taiwan Independence |
| 33. | Yü Ch'ien-ch'ang | A | 23 | Student, Yüan Lin H.S. | | | 7 | Participated in WUFI* |
| 34. | Huang Chien-jung | A | — | Naval officer | | | 2/3 | |
| 35. | Ch'en Hsien-teh | A | 38 | Primary school teacher | | | 2/3 | Plotted Taiwan Independence |
| 36. | Huang Tung-fang | A | — | Reserve military prison guard | TGC | 1969.6 | 2/1 | Plotted Taiwan Independence |
| 37. | Cheng Ming-kao | A | — | Primary school teacher | | | 7 | Passed letters for jailed F.I. elements |
| 38. | Chang-yang Ch'ing-li | A | — | Pork seller | | | 5 | Discontented with status quo |
| 39. | Tai Jung-teh | A | — | Hydroelectrical engineer | FBI | 1968.4 | 2/3 | |
| 40. | Lin Yung-sheng | A | — | Student, Tamkang College of Arts | SS | | 5 | |
| 41. | Lo Tzu-hsüan | A | 25 | Student, Shih Chieh Tech. | SS | 1969.6 | 2/3 | |
| 42. | Li Yi-yi | A | 33 | Merchant | SS | | 5 | |
| 43. | Wu Yi-nan | A | — | Naval reserve officer | | | 2/3 | |
| 44. | Liao Teng-chu | A | — | Electrical engineer | SS | | 5 | |
| 45. | Hsieh Jung-chou | A | 21 | Lumber yard business | PD | | 7 | |
| 46. | Chang Tzu-yü | A | — | Worker, textile factory | | | 2/3 | |
| 47. | Lin T'ien-che | A | — | Tailor | | | 7 | |
| 48. | Wu Yao-chung | A | 34 | Ass't prof, Professional College of Arts | SS | | 5 | |
| 49. | Lo Wen-sung | A | 18 | Advertising | FBI | | 7 | |
| 50. | Chan Hsing-wang | A | 45 | Village elder (li chang) | | 1967 | 5 | |
| 51. | Fang Jung-huei | A | 28 | Teacher | | | 2/1 | |
| 52. | Ch'en Yü-hsi | A | 32 | Student abroad (America) | SS | 1968.9 | 2/3 | |
| 53. | Kao Po-tao | A | — | Doctor, mountain highlands | | 1969 | 5 | |
| 54. | Kao A-ming | A | 40 | Primary school teacher | | 1969 | 5 | |
| 55. | Ku Shih-chi | C | — | Accountant | FBI | 60.10.5 | 2/1 | |
| 56. | Yeh Chiang-shuei | A | 50 | Worker, Kaohsiung Steel Works | | 1960.12 | 5 | Implicate |
| 57. | Yeh Ch'eng-hsiang | A | 45 | Worker, Kaohsiung Steel Works | | 1960.12 | 5 | Implicate |
| 58. | Yü Chi-t'ien | A | 44 | Census taker, ward office | | 1960.12 | 5 | Implicate |
| 59. | Sun Jung-ts'an | A | 44 | Laborer | | 1960.12 | 5 | Implicate |
| 60. | Ou-yang Mi | C | 56 | | FBI | 1965.12 | 5 | Escaped |

A hand-written list of 214 political prisoners was secretly delivered abroad and subsequently published in *Taiwan Chinglian* magazine in Japan. *Ronin* magazine, also published in Japan, carried an English version of the same list in its December 1972 issue.

A hand-written list of 237 political prisoners, believed to have been the first such list sent overseas. It contained the names of prisoners held at Taiyuan Prison and elsewhere.

# Overseas Taiwanese: Compassion out of Fear

Before foreign human rights activists began to devote themselves to Taiwan political prisoner rescue work, overseas Taiwanese had already been making strenuous efforts to publicize the human rights situation in Taiwan. They organized groups, published magazines and pamphlets, organized activities, gave speeches, staged protests, held parades, and lobbied US congressional members. By the 1980s there were over a hundred such organizations and publications, most of which were in the US and Japan. The impact was wide and long-lasting, reaching various human rights organizations, academia, political parties, the media, and even national governments.

But there were dangers: even when living abroad, any Taiwanese bold enough to challenge the KMT regime could be monitored by secret agents and even be abducted. There were several well-known cases in the 1960s of Taiwanese studying in Japan being abducted and sent back to Taiwan. One of them, the Liu Wen-ching case, made the headlines.

R6

R7

*Taiwan Chinglian* magazine, published in Japan since the 1960s. "Chinglian" means "young people."

"Verdict of the Liu Wen-ching Case," *Taiwan Chinglian*, January 5, 1978.

R12

R13

2131 Lindsay Road
Pittsburgh, PA 15221
February 23, 1977

President Jimmy Carter
White House
Washington, D.C. 20500

Dear Mr. President:

One way to judge the greatness of a person in our society is to measure the distance between what he says and what he does. The shorter the distance, the greater the person.

Your recent letter to Professor A. D. Sakharov, demonstrating your respect for human rights, indicates that you are well on your way to historical greatness.

There are many examples of abuse of human rights in this world. I would like to call your attention to another case which is taking place in one of our allied countries, namely the Republic of China on Taiwan. Nine years ago, a brilliant intellect and outstanding journalist was secretly arrested without public trial and has been imprisoned ever since. He is a patriot and the conscience of that nation and her people. He spoke and wrote for the common people. His name is Kuo, I-tung (郭衣洞), but is better known to the public by the pen-name, Po Yang (柏楊). Attached are some documents concerning his case, including a book in Chinese, entitled *Po Yang and His Unjust Imprisonment*, edited by myself, and New York Times reports.

You will most likely not have time to look into the details of this case, so I am taking the liberty of also sending a copy of this letter to Mr. Burton Levin, Republic of China Affairs, the State Department and to Ambassador Leonard Unger at the U.S. Embassy, Taipei, in the hope that they will initiate a study of the case for you. I am also sending a copy of this letter to Senator H. John Heinz, III, of Penna. and to Representative William S. Moorhead of my district. I am sure that they too will help you and us all in fighting for human rights.

The practice of totalitarianism is not a Russian monopoly. The above case is particularly important to us because we do not want the Russians to accuse us of supporting a violation of human rights perpetrated by the government of our traditional ally.

A copy of this letter is also being sent to Congressman Charles Wilson of California, who I assume would welcome being informed of the facts which reveal a dark side of Taiwan, little known by the American

**"A Solemn Statement in Support of Taiwan's Human Rights Activists,"** published in Washington D.C. on July 1, 1978, calling on the KMT to introduce **"politics for everyone."**

**Po Yang, a reputable Taiwan writer, was arrested in 1968 and sentenced to twelve years' imprisonment. On February 23, 1977, a Taiwan scholar in the US, Sun Kuan-han, wrote a petition letter on his behalf to President Jimmy Carter.**

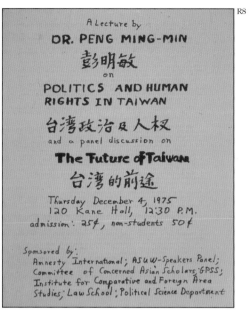

A publicity flier for a Peng Ming-min lecture at an American university.

"*Anti Political Oppression,*" booklet published in January 1977, by the Committee to Rescue Our Relatives under Oppression in Taiwan, an organization based in the California Bay Area.

This book talks about the people's life and the social and political situation under Martial Law in Taiwan.

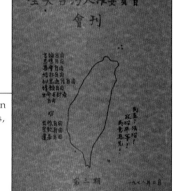

Monthly newsletter of the Formosan Association for Human Rights, February 1978.

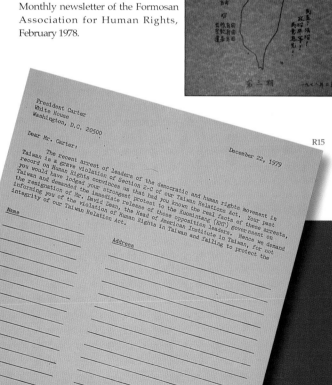

The Formosan Association for Human Rights solicited help for the victims of the Kaohsiung Incident. Their petition actions included writing letters to President Jimmy Carter, Senator Edward Kennedy, *left*, and other dignitaries. December 1979.

# Church Groups: Insistence on the Realization of Universal Rights

The church was the earliest international organization to have lent a supporting hand to Taiwan's human rights. The Presbyterian Church played a crucial role in the promotion and advancement of Taiwan's human rights. The Roman Catholic Maryknoll Order, and the American Friends Service Committee—a multiple Nobel Peace Prize winner—have both made great contributions to the human rights movement in Taiwan.

Many missionaries were also human rights activists. For example, Michael Thornberry who helped sneak out a list of Taiwan political prisoners and got it published internationally, was expelled by the KMT regime in 1971. There were more than ten missionaries who were expelled from Taiwan or restricted from entering over the ensuing decade because of their support for Taiwan's human rights movement. These included:

- Reverend Donald Wilson, assistant to the secretary general of the Presbyterian Church, expelled because of his involvement in the Hsieh Tsung-min case;
- Father Ronald Boccieri from the Maryknoll Order, who was forcibly repatriated to Ireland in 1977 for having helped hide Chen Chu, a much sought-after human rights and opposition activist;
- Reverend Daniel Beeby from the Tainan Theological College and Seminary was forced to leave Taiwan after having played an important role in the drafting of the "Statement on Our National Fate" by the Executive Committee of the PCT's General Assembly; after his return to the UK, he remained involved by assisting communication among Taiwan's human rights groups and Amnesty International.

Father Ronald Boccieri.

R16

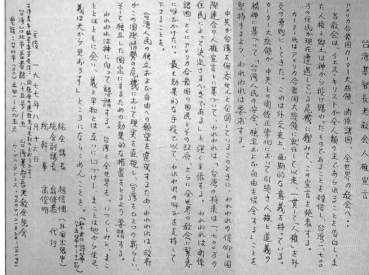
R17

The Japanese version of the "Declaration of Human Rights" by the Presbyterian Church in Taiwan, September 5, 1977.

R18

In Japan, *Christ Weekly* reported on the "Declaration on Human Rights" by the Presbyterian Church in Taiwan, April 15, 1978.

THE FUTURE OF TAIWAN

The English version of the PCT's "Statement on Our National Fate," December 29, 1971. The British Council of Churches and the Conference of British Missionary Societies also published a booklet dedicated to this cause.

R19

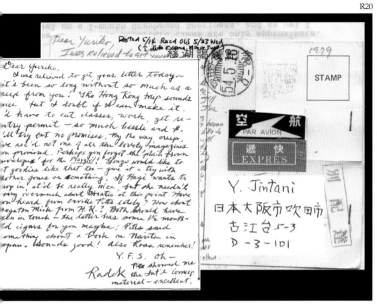

*Left*: A postcard sent from Taipei to the International Committee for the Defense of Human Rights in Taiwan, in Osaka. To avoid detection by mail inspectors, the information was written in code between the lines.

*Right*: Foreigner volunteers who acted as messengers: Elaine Lipton, *left*, and Carol Pelletier, *right*.

# Foreign Friends, Secret Rescue

From the 1970s, individuals began to get involved in underground rescue network. Using secret means, many foreign students, housewives, and foreign correspondents in Taiwan helped deliver human rights-related information abroad. By the end of the 1970s, there were several thousand people worldwide who were dedicating themselves to the cause of Taiwan's human rights. Their focus was on rights of speech and publication, as well as on the release of political prisoners.

As with the local citizens, foreigners in Taiwan faced tremendous risks in transmitting such information. Rick Ricketts, working with the US military in Taiwan, was expelled in 1971 and court-martialed because he had been caught transmitting human rights-related information abroad.

Miyake Kiyoko from Japan and Lynn Miles from the US played crucial roles in the informational "underground railroad." They circulated abroad the latest information on Taiwan's human rights situation, while staying in close contact with such human rights workers as Dr. Tien Chao-ming, Chen Chu, and Hsieh Hsiu-mei, and they maintained constant correspondence with foreign human rights volunteers in Taiwan, many of them working clandestinely. They also established regular channels of communication with overseas Taiwanese and human rights groups.

These human rights groups included Amnesty International (headquartered in London), the International Committee for the Defense of Human Rights in Taiwan (Osaka), the Taiwan Political Prisoner Rescue Association (Tokyo), the Society for the Protection of East Asian Human Rights (New York), among others. Overseas Taiwanese groups also launched activities centering on human rights. Among these expatriate groups were the Formosan Association for Human Rights (New York) and the Overseas Support for the Democratic Movement in Taiwan (Chicago), probably the two most active.

After Lynn Miles was blacklisted from entering Taiwan, he stayed in Japan as the coordinator for rescue efforts and information releases to the international press. Miyake Kiyoko, married to a Taiwanese and able to travel freely to Taiwan, was often charged with the responsibility of conveying important information abroad.

The methods of passing and carrying information were often rather creative: Miyake hid important documents inside her daughter's diapers, to secret them undetected through customs at the airport. Lynn Miles and volunteers from the International Committee for the Defense of Human Rights in Taiwan had developed a set of secret codes for postcards. They wrote down important information regarding the departure and arrival time of couriers or regarding political prisoners and sent the cards out from Taipei. Pseudonyms of the messengers and human rights volunteers were used, different from card to card, in alphabetical order. Thus, if one postcard was not delivered and went missing, they would know that things probably had gone wrong.

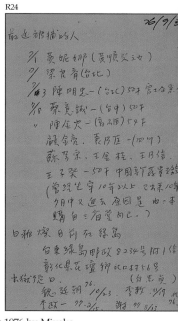

A post card sent to Lynn Miles in September 1976 by Miyake Kiyoko, in which she used the pseudonym, Ms. Chen. The content was a list of those arrested in the Chen Ming-chung case two months before.

Rosemary Haddon, *center*, a foreign student who helped deliver messages. Su Hung Yueh-chiao, *left*, wife of Su Tung-chi, at the Taiwan Provincial Assembly, circa 1978.

The Taiwan Communiqué, first published on December 10, 1980, has remained devoted to Taiwan issues for over two decades, and is still being published by its founders, Gerrit and Mei-chin van der Wees.

August 19, 1978 newsletter published by the Taiwan Political Prisoner Rescue Association in Japan, reporting the arrest of Chen Chu.

Petition on behalf of Lin Yi-hsiung by Japan's International Committee for the Defense of Human Rights in Taiwan, 1981.

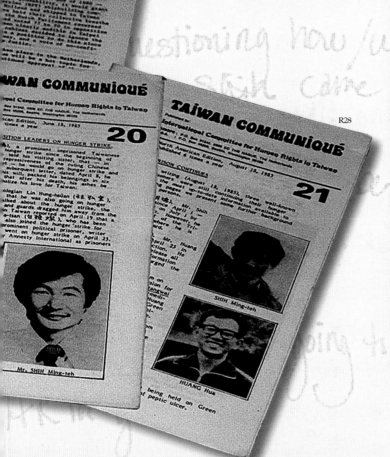

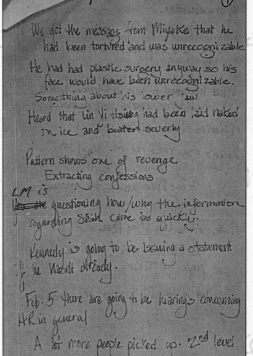

January 1981 notes made by Carol Pelletier. She wrote: "heard that Lin Yi-hsiung had been laid naked on ice and beaten severely."

# Amnesty International: Global Actions throughout the Years

Amnesty International (AI) was first established in 1961 in the UK. In 1977, this internationally recognized organization was awarded the Nobel Peace Prize to honor its contribution to human rights worldwide. To investigate the political prisoner and general human rights situations, its secretary general, Martin Ennals, paid two visits to Taiwan between 1969 and 1970.

Between 1975 and 1979, AI dispatched many teams to Taiwan to investigate cases of human rights abuse and to observe related trials. AI also maintained close contact with active overseas members working on Taiwan's human rights. AI's International Secretariat published the results of its investigation and sent these findings to its sections and groups all over the world, while mobilizing its members globally to pressure the KMT regime and to demand unconditional release of political prisoners (prisoners of conscience). AI being a highly reputable international human rights organization, it was difficult for the KMT regime to ignore or refute its human rights reports.

AI rescue actions took on many forms. Some examples:

- Mobilizing AI members to write letters of appeal to the heads of state or ministers of justice in countries with oppressive human rights records;
- Exerting pressure on national governments and legislatures to intervene in human rights situations of neighboring countries or countries with close diplomatic ties;
- Extending long-term support to political prisoners and their family members by writing letters to prisons, arranging prison visits, providing financial assistance to family members, etc.;
- Sending lawyers or human rights workers to monitor political trials.

R29

AI's London headquarters dispatched vice-chair of its Japan Section, Prof. Nishikawa Toshiyuki, *center*, to observe the trial of Yu Teng-fa on March 9, 1979 at the Taiwan Garrison Command military court. *From left*, human rights workers Chen Chu and Tien Chiu-chin. *Right*, democracy fighter Su Chiu-chen.

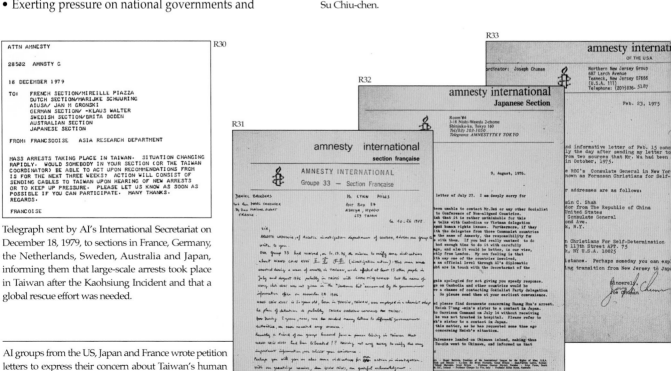

Telegraph sent by AI's International Secretariat on December 18, 1979, to sections in France, Germany, the Netherlands, Sweden, Australia and Japan, informing them that large-scale arrests took place in Taiwan after the Kaohsiung Incident and that a global rescue effort was needed.

AI groups from the US, Japan and France wrote petition letters to express their concern about Taiwan's human rights.

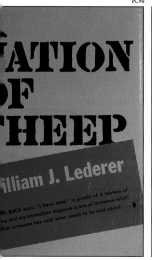

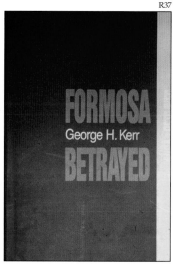

R34 R35 R36 R37

# International Press:
# Publicizing the Truth of Taiwan's Human Rights Situation

During the Cold War era, apart from a few left-wing media, most international press organizations showed little interest, and even fewer carried articles critical of the KMT regime. Major international media groups did not have correspondents in Taiwan at that time. Instead, stringers were hired—usually locals, who had to be extra cautious in reporting on human rights-related issues.

George H. Kerr's *Formosa Betrayed*, published in 1966, contained a great many details of the February 28 Incident, and its impact has exceeded all other such books on Taiwanese history. In 1961 William J. Lederer, who co-authored the American best-seller *The Ugly American*, published *A Nation of Sheep*, in which he devoted a

chapter to the KMT's rule of terror. At a time of prevailing MaCarthyism and anti-communist sentiment in the US, the "Free China" myth of the KMT regime was supported by the US government. *Formosa Betrayed* and *A Nation of Sheep* were timely publications that penetrated such lies.

*A Taste of Freedom* by Peng Ming-min, *Taiwan's 400 Year History* by Su Ming (Su Beng), and other books were also a great source of inspiration to foreigners. The weekly *Far Eastern Economic Review* often dedicated special coverage to Taiwan's political situation. Journalists such as Melinda Liu, Bill Armbruster and Bill Kazer wrote many articles in the 1970s, introducing the Tangwai movement to the international community.

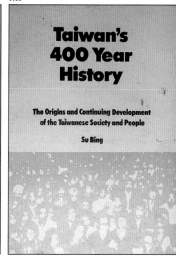

R38 R39 R40 R41

Besides the publications of human rights groups, there were some limited-circulation alternative publications such as *Ronin* in Japan (published in December 1972, with attached list of political prisoners, see p. 141), *The Seventies* in Hong Kong, *AMPO*, *Monsoon* and *Asian Eye*. Although they issued the most severe criticism of the KMT government, their readership was limited to mostly left-wing liberals.

# Official Organizations and Academia:
# Tremendous Pressure on the KMT Regime

After the mid-1970s, the US Congress often held public hearings on Taiwan's human rights situation. Minnesota Congressman Donald Fraser was the first congressional member to be involved in Taiwan's human rights issues and made great contributions in this regard. There were also some university and college professors who were active in advocating Taiwan's human rights. Some even took part in petitioning and other human rights campaign activities. For example:

- Professor James Seymour of Columbia University;
- Professor Richard Kagan of Hamline University;
- University of Hawaii, which expressed concern over the arrest of one of its students, Chen Yu-hsi (1971);
- Carnegie Mellon University, which expressed concern over the mysterious death of one of its professors, Chen Wen-chen (1981).

R42

Chen Yu-hsi, a student at University of Hawaii, was charged by the KMT regime with "reading the works of Mao Zedong in the university library." In 1968, he was arrested in Tokyo and was forcibly repatriated to Taiwan. The University of Hawaii held the view that Chen's reading of books in its library was a free–speech right, and that accordingly he should not have been charged. Therefore, the university sent representatives to Taiwan to express concern. Under such international pressure, Chen's trial was conducted openly and he was sentenced to seven years of imprisonment.

R43

The University of Hawaii *International Students Newsletter* reported on how its students from Taiwan were being monitored by KMT secret agents, November 6, 1978.

R44

### TAIWAN AGENTS IN AMERICA AND THE DEATH OF PROF. WEN-CHEN CHEN

**HEARINGS**

BEFORE THE

SUBCOMMITTEES ON
ASIAN AND PACIFIC AFFAIRS
AND ON
HUMAN RIGHTS AND
INTERNATIONAL ORGANIZATIONS
OF THE
COMMITTEE ON FOREIGN AFFAIRS
HOUSE OF REPRESENTATIVES
NINETY-SEVENTH CONGRESS
FIRST SESSION

JULY 30 AND OCTOBER 6, 1981

Printed for the use of the Committee on Foreign Affairs

U.S. GOVERNMENT PRINTING OFFICE
WASHINGTON : 1982

R45

### MARTIAL LAW ON TAIWAN AND UNITED STATES FOREIGN POLICY INTERESTS

**HEARING**

BEFORE THE

SUBCOMMITTEE ON
ASIAN AND PACIFIC AFFAIRS
OF THE
COMMITTEE ON FOREIGN AFFAIRS
HOUSE OF REPRESENTATIVES
NINETY-SEVENTH CONGRESS
SECOND SESSION

MAY 20, 1982

Printed for the use of the Committee on Foreign Affairs

U.S. GOVERNMENT PRINTING OFFICE
WASHINGTON : 1982

*Left*: Two US congressional hearings were held on the Chen Wen-chen case (July and October 1981) . Witnesses included Chen's widow, Chen Su-chen, Representative Jim Leach from Iowa, and Richard Cyert, president of Carnegie Mellon University.

*Right*: US congressional hearing on Martial Law on Taiwan, May 20, 1982.

R46

東亞人权協会会長司馬晉的發言

去年秋天，台灣當局決定对反抗力量採取高压政策。 江南的謀殺案件大家熟知。雖然我們不確定那些官員应负最後責任，但我們確实知道那几位官員应对在謀殺案的第三天在一次秘密会議中所做的決定負責。在這次警總秘密会議中，他們討論如何加強文宣檢工作，加強控制思想与消息的傳播。用他們的術語本説，是從「消極」被動的政策轉变为「積極」主動的措施。雖然這項決定因為江南案件引起国際上的抗議而暫为延期，但两星期前終於付之实行。

施明德絕食就是对去年秋天以來政府剝夺人民基本权利的一項抗議。不問我們是否同意他的政治主張，我們十分支持他為保護人权所做的努力。

我們深信這項努力最終达到它的目的。目的。

我呼吁台灣當局不再踌躇当机立断,立刻釋放所有良心因犯、并充分尊重言論自由、解除報禁。

1985 5月18日

STATEMENT BY JAMES SEYMOUR TO NEW YORK RALLY IN SUPPORT OF SHIH MING-TEH, MAY 18, 1985.

Last autumn, the authorities on Taiwan decided to embark on a course of heavy repression.
The murder of Henry Liu is well known. Although we do not know which officials bear ultimate responsibility for this act, we do know who were responsible for certain decisions taken the very next day, at a secret meeting of the Taiwan Garrison Command, et al. At that meeting, the authorities planned a switch from (to use their terminology) "passive" to "active" in controlling the ideas and information which the people of Taiwan are allowed to read and hear. Apparently because of the international furor over the murder of Henry Liu, the escalation of censorship was postponed, but the plan went into effect two weeks ago.
Mr. Shih's hunger strike has in large part been a reaction to the government's decisions of last fall to go even further in denying the people of Taiwan their human rights. Whether or not we agree with all of his political views, we stand solidly behind his effort to promote human rights for Taiwan. I am convinced that is the long run this effort will prevail.
I call upon the authorities on Taiwan to delay no longer, immediately release all prisoners of conscience, and end press censorship.

Professor James Seymour's Society for the Protection of East Asian Human Rights released his hand-written statement, calling on the KMT regime to immediately release all prisoners of conscience, May 18, 1985.

R47

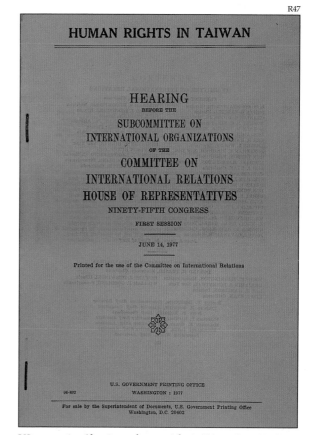

### HUMAN RIGHTS IN TAIWAN

**HEARING**

BEFORE THE

SUBCOMMITTEE ON
INTERNATIONAL ORGANIZATIONS
OF THE
COMMITTEE ON
INTERNATIONAL RELATIONS
HOUSE OF REPRESENTATIVES
NINETY-FIFTH CONGRESS
FIRST SESSION

JUNE 14, 1977

Printed for the use of the Committee on International Relations

U.S. GOVERNMENT PRINTING OFFICE
94-892 WASHINGTON : 1977

For sale by the Superintendent of Documents, U.S. Government Printing Office
Washington, D.C. 20402

US congressional hearing on human rights in Taiwan, June 14, 1977.

Human Rights Activists Speak—I

# How Long the Road?

**by Lynn Miles**

I first came to Taiwan days before the harvest moon of 1962, with the cold war raging full bore on this, the eastern front. Close friends, my host family where I first stayed, my university teachers and staff—Mainlanders one and all. Many came from military or diplomatic families, each in their own way critical cogs in the political, military and intelligence apparatus described in these pages. For example, the "Dad" in my family had once, while still on the mainland, been a close aide of the dreaded Tai Li, and after coming to Taiwan was first at the helm of the newly established National Security Bureau. No wonder, then, that at first I did not doubt the image of Taiwan that the government was intent on presenting to the world: in my mind as in just about everyone else's, "Formosa" had now become "Free China."

### Free China or Formosa betrayed?

All that changed with my second trip here, in 1965. A rude awakening came upon reading George H.Kerr's *Formosa Betrayed* and William Lederer's *A Nation of Sheep*, two seminal early-sixties exposés. Their revelations, which treated a history so modern as to be current, did not at all jibe with the official story. I was getting an inkling of the dark, unreported side of Taiwan politics and social life.

When I proceeded to test the veracity of these unflattering reports by questioning my closest friends (who were by this time not confined to Mainlanders), I gradually had them confirmed – always in whispered, surreptitious tones. One of my classmates, from the Tainan countryside, told of an uncle who disappeared one night and never came back. Private conversations only added detail to the bloody Kerr-Lederer accounts. I was afire with indignation, not only because the whispers suggested a national secret not to be shared with foreigners, but also because as an American I felt

responsible for "my" government's role as prop for the KMT, whose support was otherwise lacking.

One thing led to another. Soon I was reading Lee Ao's *Monologue Under Tradition*, a hot item in the Taiwan of that day (before it was banned, in 1966). Taking an immediate fancy to the pluck with which he lambasted corruption in academia and high government places, I shot off a fan letter to this "Mark Twain of modern China." We soon became friends, and I would visit his place every couple of months for a schooling of the kind that you cannot get in school. Our association brought me up to speed on the dirty, hidden, unwritten history of the KMT government, both before and after it took refuge on Taiwan.

With the arrest of Lee Ao, Hsieh Tsung-min and Wei Ting-chao in early 1971, my historical abstractions became present realities. For the crime of consorting with such out-of-favor friends, I was expelled from Taiwan, not to be de-blacklisted until 1996.

My first decade beyond the pale was spent in Osaka, where I worked to get materials about the political prisons and the people who filled them into the hands of journalists, church groups, Amnesty International and other such human rights organizations. With time, the circle of those interested in political prisoner rescue work grew, as our coterie of like-minded activists linked up with the underground network in Taiwan and its globe-girdling counterpart.

Commitment to this decades-long human rights campaign came neither all at once nor as part of a well-defined, rational train of thought. Rather, it was a series of small and seemingly inconsequential steps taken under the press of circumstances. You might say that by degrees I was just sucked into it. Little did I imagine that I would be so changed. This was partly the consequence of seeing those around me changing, and the world changing, in the direction

S1

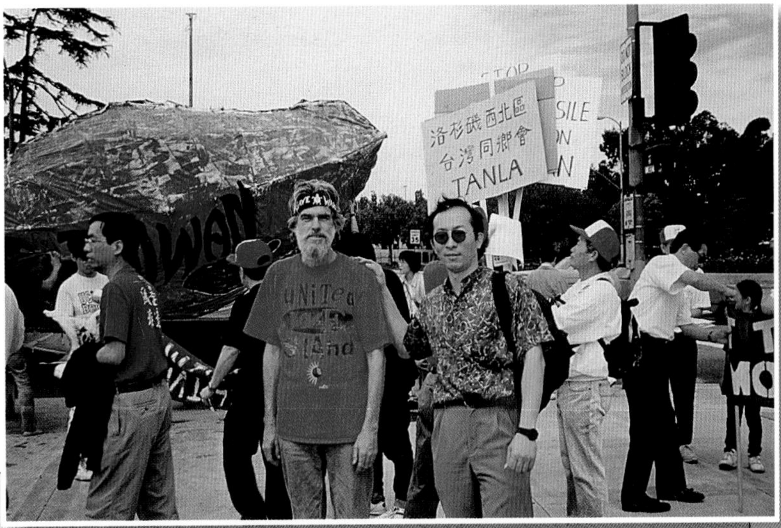

Lynn Miles, in red T-shirt, was an important coordinator for the overseas rescue network. He was listed as persona non grata by the KMT regime and was forbidden from entering Taiwan from 1971 to 1996.

Lynn Miles' letter to Professor James Seymour of Columbia University, giving him instructions on how to pass information to dissident Chen Ku-ying, how to meet with oppositionist Wu San-lien and how to use the secret codes to access important contacts.

SYMOUR

Message for Mrs. Chen Ku-ying: plase come thru Osaka on way out.

China News of 3/18 says a policeman sentenced to death for extortion.

Minchung Daily was reorganized for reporting of K Incident?

Meet Wu San-lien, ask story behind his letter to Kuo Yu-hsin.

Any comp-ehensive eyewitness report of K Incident written inside Taiwan?

Lin Yi-hsiung has written a book. Can you find a way to get it out, both to USA, Japan and HK?

Someone will probably be going to Taiwan in the next week or so. ~~He will phone you and use the name "Niwa," if Japanese, or~~ Courier for things coming out. He will call you and address you as "JS," and you answer "This is he." He will say that he is waiting for you downstairs, but will actually be waiting in the Hilton Hotel coffeeshop.

Fountain RR sta. visual contact – after started from 1 mile se – follow you into Rest. 30 min later. Dirty blond. ~~Button-down pocket.~~ My friend Reading ch. News. Short hair.

S2

of a heightened concern for shared universal values. People of heart, imagination, courage and generosity are treasures each and every one; thanks to them the work became all the more transformative. That is to say, commitment, while not coming all at once, certainly came easily.

Why was getting accurate and timely information into the hands of journalists and people of conscience abroad our first mission? Because, having silenced the opposition at home, what the Chiang regime feared most was censure in the court of international opinion—"bad press" in places where public opinion still factored in public policy-making. The whole "Free World" fabric was nothing but a subtle and intricate tissue of lies, prejudices and chauvinistic conceits that had to be maintained at any cost; the major media was little interested in publishing anything that might prove embarrassing to the United States or its client regimes. So, getting the Chiang family some "bad press" was not the easiest of assignments.

Take the arrest of Chen Chu in 1978. For me, it meant hurriedly translating and copying background materials, then hopping on the Bullet Express to Tokyo, there to buttonhole whomever might be hanging out at the Japan Foreign Correspondents Club. Of the dozen or so reporters that I cornered, only one, Robert Whymant of the *London Guardian*, showed the slightest interest. The others begged off with the oft-heard excuse that any story they might write would not get past their editor back home. When we consider that at that time Chen Chu already had a reputation as a courageous fighter for press freedom, and yet her arrest was not worth international note in the eyes of these molders of public opinion, we begin to see the enormity of the problem. With such dogged indifference being the normal approach to "objective journalism," it was hard to believe that someday, somehow, efforts to get the public spotlight squarely trained on human rights abuses would pay off. In fact, keeping faith was the hardest challenge of all.

## Dogged indifference meets the collective mind

Nonetheless, there was progress, however prosaic. By the end of the seventies, the U.S. administration under Jimmy Carter had begun applying a human rights yardstick to American foreign policy. Coming into office in January 1977, he wasted no time in putting one veteran civil rights activist in charge of the newly founded human rights office in the State Department, while choosing another as UN ambassador. Carter was unable to stay the course, however, and by the middle of his term was barely going through the motions, more often not even doing that much. But the idea had already caught hold globally that client regimes could no longer wantonly trample on their subjects' rights without being brought to account. Amnesty International's winning of the Nobel Peace Prize in 1977 was a reflection of this trend (and one that gave us immense encouragement). Other agencies weighed into the fray….

What was being called "the court of international opinion" was beginning to matter mightily to oppressor and oppressed alike, for the first battlefield in this protracted war was in the landscape of the mind—the collective mind.

Today Carter often gets credit for "leading" the

movement to break the cozy ties between the U.S. and its repressive clients, of which there many. But I prefer to think that he came to power at a time when, unlike now, democracy in the U.S. was working after a fashion, and popular revulsion at U.S. spoon-feeding of dictators was actually registering in Washington. Carter was not so much leading the wave, as following it.

Today it is fashionable to say of Taiwan that human rights, freedom and democracy have been "achieved," as if all that were needed to decide the question was for the electorate to send a democrat into the Presidential Office. Sorry to say, the matter is never resolved. Yes, we've come a long way from those dark decades when extra mileage had to be teased from a whispered remark or subtle play on words. And who can ignore the politicians who play rambunctious ruffians in the legislature by day and TV talking heads by night? Aren't they proof positive that anyone can make the most outlandish anti-government accusations without fear of a midnight visit from some black hand?

The answer is "yes" without a doubt. But many human rights problems still go begging for solution. First, all that nuclear waste foisted on a powerless minority on Pongso-no-Tao is still there, notwithstanding DPP promises to remove it. Second, not only is the death penalty still with us, the DPP has even tried to expand its coverage, saying that this is a "world trend" (no matter that Amnesty International says otherwise). Third, white slavery still flourishes, from the Taipei metropolis to the backwater township. Fourth, labor rights, especially for foreigners, rate little attention in a land mesmerized by the economic miracle. Fifth, secret-police activities like photographing of demonstrators followed up by visits to their employers, phone-tapping of dissidents, and more still reckon as important tools of intimidation, reading like a page out of some Martial Law-era training manual. So, while a retrospective look at the nightmare of the February 28 Incident and the White Terror give some indication of the ground we have covered, they hardly answer the question, How far yet to go?

In truth the question is unanswerable anyway. Even if Taiwanese have become masters of their own political system, there is still a very powerful international dynamic that continually impinges on domestic consciousness and freedom of action. Just as the postwar repression in Taiwan lasting well into the eighties worked as part of a larger transnational dynamic, likewise the opposition to it transcended state-imposed borders. The same holds true today. One's destiny is not entirely in one's own hands.

## Martial law, then and now, here and there

When Chen Shui-bian offers up hackneyed homilies about "freedom" and "democracy" in the U.S. (as he did recently to the UN-based reporters in New York), he disappoints those human rights activists who cannot ignore the arrests—within days of his speech—of many hundreds of people for peacefully demonstrating on the streets of that very city. Nor can they ignore the hundreds more who are still now, two years and more after their secret arrest, being denied legal representation, family visitation rights, the right to know the charges against them, and the right to face their accusers in open court. All of this enjoys the sanction of the Patriot Act, a latter-day clone of Taiwan's draconian Martial Law measures of yesteryear. Hearing A-bian talk like this, who among civil libertarians does not grimace at the notion of calling Taiwan's president an ally in the fight for human rights?

And finally, there is the problem of nationalism, whether it takes the form of questing for a United China or yearning for an Independent Taiwan. Proponents are forever attributing the most sinister of motives to their opposites on the other side of the ideological divide. Many in the pan-blue camp see the pan-greens as tools of the Americans pure and simple, while the pan-greens are just as certain that the pan-blues are in bed with the Chinese Communists. One views the other as bellicose bordering on insane, neither will credit the other with having arrived at their "national identity" legitimately. In this blue-vs-green, not-so-cold cold war, one is pressed to declare allegiances loud and clear. Failure to take sides means being sidelined altogether.

But if there's nothing wrong with loving Taiwan with all of its faults, what's the problem with loving China with all of its faults? Are respect for Taiwan, respect for America, and respect for China mutually exclusive? Does adoration for one parent negate that for the other? Does love for one child mean that the other must go without?

If we are truly willing to march confidently into the future to the beat of the idealist drummer, if we are unafraid to push the envelope on our evolving definition of "human rights," let us quit hating altogether, and start treating our intellectual rivals as worthies and—far from fighting them—seek win-win solutions.

This road has no horizon. Today, sixty-odd years later and with over one hundred million lives lost in the meantime in chasing after the promises of the pre-Pearl Harbor Atlantic Charter, Taiwan beckons as the potential mother of all ground zeroes. Notwithstanding such negative signposts, and no matter how long the road and no matter how rocky, we must stay the course. Our children and their hopes and dreams depend on it. Nothing has changed. Now as then, only courage and faith will meet the challenge, no matter how long the road.

Human Rights Activists Speak—II

# What Could I Do for Them?

by Miyake Kiyoko

I lived in Taiwan in the late sixties and early seventies. Having declaring Martial Law in 1949, Taiwan entered a long period of opposition to China in the international arena, while at home it was an age of terror featuring the suppression of human rights, prohibition of citizens' political activities, deprivation of their basic human rights, and mass arrests leading to political imprisonment.

And yet, during this period of Martial Law, magazines and other mass media made Taiwan seem a pleasant place to live. At the time, anywhere between five and six hundred thousand Japanese tourists came to Taiwan, whether on business or to pursue sexual favors. No matter their purpose, none of them dared face the basic facts about Taiwan: that the Kuomintang was a one-party dictatorship; that with "retake the mainland" being sung from on high, secret police could be found in every corner of the country; and that anyone who voiced even the slightest criticism of the government could be tagged as a communist spy or as pro-independence, and given a harsh prison sentence.

## Activist with a toothbrush

My first direct contact with such politics of terror came when I met two political prisoners released not long before, Hsieh Tsung-min and Wei Ting-chao. Both of them had joined Professor Peng Ming-min in drafting the "Declaration of Taiwan People's Self-Salvation." It was from them that I first heard the true facts of political imprisonment. Not long afterwards, Professor Peng slipped out of the country, and in 1971 Hsieh and Wei were mysteriously re-arrested, even though they had been under strict observation by the secret police the whole time.

Before that, Hsieh, who was already aware of the danger, entrusted to my safekeeping a copy of *Taiwan Chinglian* and a list of political prisoners, all wrapped in a newspaper. Upon learning of his arrest, I immediately transcribed a copy of the list, and had a returning Japanese diplomat take it back to Japan. Without being informed of its contents, he forwarded it to the publishers of *Taiwan Chinglian*. And then I immediately became active, trying to learn the current situation of the political prisoners' families, whom I contacted using the original list that I still had with me.

A better understanding of the sad plight of the prisoners led me to consider the question of what I could do for them. Ultimately the answer came that I should strive to uncover the truth and let international society know about it. KMT repression of human rights would only be attenuated through international pressure, so there was no other course open.

I am often asked, "How is it that a Japanese woman all alone in Taiwan had the courage to work to rescue political prisoners, whom everyone else was afraid to support?" But it was precisely because I was Japanese that I was able to undertake rescue work. The same endeavor, if undertaken by a Taiwanese, could mean arrest or even execution. I thought that a foreigner enjoyed relatively more room for rescue work, and what's more I had a channel that made contact with the outside possible, so I believed that only I was capable of doing it.

That said, this was still an extremely dangerous activity, and I was unable to call on anyone else for help. So all I could do was steel myself and plunge forward. At that time there was the term "toothbrushism" to lampoon those high KMT government officials and financial lords who would use their privileges and corruption to enrich themselves and move their families out of the country, transferring their assets along with them—at the first sign of trouble they could grab their toothbrush and flee.

I was also a "toothbrushist," but the difference was that I was destined for political prison. I was mentally prepared for the arrest that could come at any time, and had prepared my toothbrush and a change of clothes. I had also arranged for the care of my young daughter.

When Chiang Kai-shek died in 1975, some political prisoners had their sentences reduced through the amnesty and were released. I asked them who was still in prison and what prison conditions were like. Some suffered health effects that lingered after their tortures, while others, who hailed from the mainland, were impoverished and without anyone to rely on. I passed on to their friends and families medical supplies and contributions that had been collected each time I

returned to Japan. At the time, an American in Japan, Lynn Miles, was able to inform Amnesty International and people around the world about Taiwan's political prisoners. Other than that, WUFI contributed no small measure of money and medical supplies.

Taiwanese friends with whom I cooperated included, in the early years, Chen Ku-ying, the so-called "master of unification," Chen Ying-chen, who had just been released, Chen Yu-hsi, and Li Tsuo-cheng, who were later joined by Chen Chu and Tien Chao-ming. They reacted positively to my activities, and expressed a willingness to help me.

Together we set about our rescue work. At the time there was no divide between the pro-unification and pro-independence people. These people took a humanist position and strove for the release of political prisoners suffering in terrible conditions. They took my place in meeting with the ones still incarcerated, or they forwarded money to the families of the prisoners, while at the same time providing lots of information from inside prison, which I was able to send abroad.

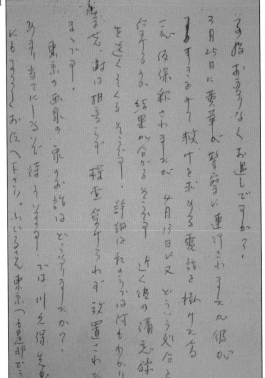

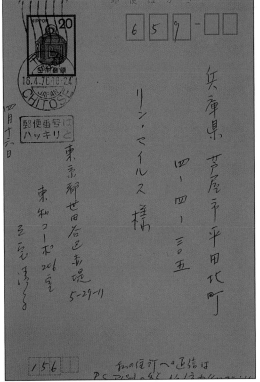

This April 1976 postcard from Miyake Kiyoko in Tokyo to Lynn Miles in Osaka reports the police detention of Huang Hua on March 25. She says that he won temporary release, and that how his case was to be handled was probably decided on April 13.

But later, the KMT authorities found out about my rescue work because I was ratted on by a certain family, and because of a certain American woman friend who was reckless and acted without careful consideration. A secret police agent approached me, feigning eagerness to help in human rights rescue work. As a result, my house was broken into and searched in the middle of the night by MPs and plainclothesmen. One time I went to the Foreign Affairs Police to extend my visa, whereupon I was detained in the basement, their intent being to force me to take ROC citizenship. The authorities even found out about my meetings with families of the political prisoners and the secret codes used when I contacted them by phone.

## Establishing a Tokyo-based rescue organization

My worries were that if I were arrested, many of those who had helped me would be implicated, and the channel for passing on information about the political prisoners would be destroyed. Naturally I would also be unable to protect my daughter. After giving the matter a lot of thought, I decided to return to Japan in 1976. Before leaving, I carefully decided on my successor, and cautiously decided on the method of contact to be used in the future.

Of international organizations in Japan working for the rescue of Taiwan's political prisoners, there was only Amnesty International working for the release of prisoners of conscience—those who had been imprisoned for their political ideals or for religious reasons. Before me, intelligence coming out of Taiwan had been indirectly passed on to AI's London headquarters, and if a political prisoner was sentenced to death, immediate action would be taken to apply massive pressure on the KMT government.

But AI's European approach to human rights was incapable of resolving the problem of political imprisonment in Asia. And AI's Japan section was following directives from the London headquarters—fundamentally unable to understand or to thoroughly grasp the important issues of political imprisonment in Taiwan. Understanding the terrible reality of Taiwan's domestic situation, I was especially dissatisfied with AI's approach. I strongly hoped for the establishment of an organization exclusively devoted to rescuing Taiwan's political prisoners.

Fortunately, the Taiwan Political Prisoner Rescue Association was established in Tokyo in 1977, while in the Kansai area, AI's Group Five handled Taiwanese political prisoners.

The core membership of the TPPRA was people associated with UNESCO, with the Lin Kei-mei Support Association, and with the church. They had all sorts of reasons for joining, including:

1. those who joined out of atonement for wrongs committed by Japan during its colonial rule of Taiwan (1895~1945), during which time they lived there;

2. those who joined to rescue those who had been imprisoned for their leftist ideas—the people who not only wanted to resist the Chiang regime but also believed that the hope of the Taiwan people lay in "liberation by China";

3. Taiwan Independence supporters who felt that one of the tasks of the TI movement was to rescue the political prisoners regarded as enemies by the Chiang regime;

4. those church people who participated based on the Christian precepts of justice and a humanist spirit, or those who were associated with the Formosan Presbyterian Church, whose concern for human rights had invited government repression;

5. those who, based on humanitarian principles, thoroughly opposed any repression of human rights.

The TPPRA directed its appeals at the Japanese people. It held all kinds of meetings, including sending protest statements or petitions to the Taiwan authorities, as well as demonstrations in front of the Asian Relations Association (Taiwan's diplomatic presence in Tokyo), street demonstrations, hunger strikes, protests, and leaflet distribution. To raise concern about Taiwan, it published *Northwest Rain*, in which such topics as former Taiwanese soldiers who had fought for the Japanese, Taiwanese poets, and even such "soft topics" as Taiwan cuisine, were presented for a general audience. Not only this, we also kept sending people to Taiwan to get a better understanding of the situation there and especially to bring back political prisoner-related information.

At the time, conservative elements within Japanese society were in cahoots with the KMT, while the mass media, mindful of China's concerns, gave practically

One section of the 500km-long human chain. Behind the hands is a memorial plaque, located near the Yuanhuan Circle in Taipei, commemorating the outbreak of the February 28 Incident nearby.

T3

no coverage to Taiwan. Meanwhile the so-called leftist and progressive literati would, notwithstanding their concern for the Vietnam War or political prisoners in South Korea, turn a blind eye to Taiwan, ignoring the struggle for democracy, the fight against dictatorship, the bloodshed, the prison sentences, and the murders. In Japan of that time, it was truly difficult to wage a campaign for the rescue of political prisoners in Taiwan.

## Truth Investigation Commission needed now

Today that era is long gone. Taiwan has gradually democratized. From the single-party dictatorship of the Kuomintang, to the direct election by the people of the Chen Shui-bian regime in 2000, Taiwan has finally achieved its first transfer of power. The Japanese media nonetheless coldly characterize this as a case of "a trouble-maker becoming president," completely ignoring the heartfelt hopes of the Taiwan people. The Japanese media do not admit the huge significance of this kind of change, which symbolizes Taiwan's farewell to the politics of darkness.

So it was such a delight to learn that a human rights retrospective was being held in the Presidential Building, once the apex of the repressive apparatus, just as it gave me the greatest joy to join with Taiwanese on February 28, 2004 in creating a human

chain. I saw this eye-dazzling display of people standing up—the same Taiwanese who were once, in the KMT era, usually too frightened and intimidated to express their views. Now they were proudly proclaiming YES to Taiwan and NO to China, in a 500km-long chain that left no gaps all the way from the north end of Taiwan to the south.

Our faith in ongoing democratization was reconfirmed on March 20, when Chen Shui-bian was reelected to the highest office. Strong feelings that the Taiwanese did not want to again return to the dark ages led Chen to victory, however slim the margin.

I congratulate Chen Shui-bian on his assumption of a second term. Yet, as one once involved in the rescue and support of political prisoners, I would also like to express my strongest desire concerning the events of February 28 and the White Terror that followed, in which so many people were killed by the KMT regime. According to the survivors and the families of the victims, the facts are gradually becoming clear, but on the side of the victimizers, there has been virtually no attempt to seek out the truth or assign blame. Victim has not been matched to victimizer. If a Truth Investigation Commission is established, then the deeds and names of the victimizers will come to light, and they will have to take responsibility for what they did. This is what is needed to bring peace to the souls of those whose lives were lost.

T4

This happy crowd has assembled atop the famous bridge in central Taiwan, the Hsiluo Bridge, which crosses the Chuoshui River.

## Two Million Link Hands to Protect Taiwan

Addressing the crisis presented by more than 500 missiles targeting Taiwan from across the strait, two million Taiwanese form a line stretching five hundred kilometers from Taiwan's northern end to the south. On February 28, 2004, the 57th anniversary of the February 28 Incident, they broke the world record for human chains, declaring their resolution to safeguard their homeland.

The "228 Hand-in-Hand Rally" movement to link hands to protect Taiwan had the slogan "Oppose missiles, love peace!" It was a festive occasion exhibiting a great variety of inspiration and creativity, as people entertained themselves and others while showing the power of their collective strength.

T5

T6

"I love you and we love her."

The northern end of the human chain was at Peace Island, Keelung.

Logo of 228 Hand-in-Hand Rally    T7

# Like a Bird on a Wire

The nestlings call in vain for their mother. Snatched out of her nest, restrained by force, the adult bird nevertheless remains defiant. For the sake of the children, she keeps head up and chest out, ready to meet her unknown and tragic fate.

Painted by Auyang Wen

Human Rights Prospect I

# National Human Rights Policy

## Building a human rights nation and realizing universal values

Democratization is a continuous process and must be constantly deepened and consolidated, particularly in a young democracy like Taiwan. Therefore, shortly after his inauguration as president—the first-ever transfer of political power in the country, Chen Shui-bian proposed the goal of "building a human rights nation." Based on this policy, a series of human rights policy plans and their mechanisms, implementation methods, timetables, and guidelines were proposed.

### I. Basic Concept

Build a human rights state, with emphasis on meeting international human rights standards and keeping pace with international human rights developments. In addition, the protection and promotion of human rights must be made the rationale for a restored constitutional democracy.

### II. Planning, Implementation and Coordination

1. Presidential Human Rights Advisory Group
2. Executive Yuan Human Rights Protection and Promotion Committee

## III. Goals and Considerations

1. Having gone through almost half a century of authoritarian rule and thirty-eight years of martial law, Taiwan's constitutional democracy has yet to permeate into the everyday lives of its citizens. Constitutional democracy can only be restored and secured if the rule of law is observed and human rights ideas are embodied in domestic laws. Furthermore, human rights should be made the guiding principle in the democratization process.

2. In the postwar "age of human rights," the rights to which humankind are entitled are no longer limited to those stipulated by and protected by national constitutions, but should include all universal rights prescribed in international human rights instruments.

3. Forced to withdraw from the United Nations in 1971, Taiwan was also cut off from the international human rights regime. For over thirty years, she has not been able to keep pace with international human rights developments, and hence her human rights knowledge and practice have not followed world trends. The formation of policies and action plans to realize the goal of building a "human rights nation" sends a very clear message to the world community, that Taiwan, despite being isolated internationally, is still a member of the global village and is willing to take action to shoulder her rightful responsibility in the protection and realization of universal rights.

## IV. Implementation

1. Establishment of a National Human Rights Commission in accordance with the Paris Principles (draft bills of the Organic Law of National Human Rights Commission and the Law Governing the Exercise of Duties and Responsibilities of the National Human Rights Commission are pending review at the Legislative Yuan).

2. Ratification of the International Covenant on Civil and Political Rights and the International Covenant on Economic, Social and Cultural Rights, which were signed by the government in 1967 and are yet to be ratified (now still under review at the Legislative Yuan.

3. Incorporation of the aforementioned two covenants into domestic law (a Human Rights Basic Law has been drafted and is currently under review at the Executive Yuan.

4. Preparation of a National Human Rights Action Plan in accordance with the 1993 Vienna Declaration and Program of Action, with nationwide consultation.

5. Survey of the administration, including ministries and commissions under the executive branch, to examine whether they accord with constitutional and international human rights standards (phase one completed.

6. Human rights education and training (a Human Rights Education Committee under the Ministry of Education has already been established; the Organic Law of National Human Rights Memorial Museum is under review at the Legislative Yuan.

7. Acceleration and expansion of exchange and cooperation with international human rights organizations.

8. Publication of the first-ever National Human Rights Report (March 2003).

*This section is a summary based on information in the 2002 Human Rights Policy White Paper and other materials released by the Presidential Human Rights Advisory Group, the Executive Yuan's Human Rights Protection and Promotion Committee and other related agencies. Updated 2004.*

## Human Rights Prospect II

# Reflection
# and Remembrance

## A New Trend: Peace Museums

Since the end of the Second World War, museums and memorials commemorating the past have become common around the globe. Furthermore, starting from the beginning of the 1980s, peace museums focusing on some incident or massacre, war or peace, or the twentieth-century struggle for human rights have signaled a new wave in museum design. These museums use the more microspective and folk-history approach to storytelling, in order to better render the truth of history in all its diversity. Directions in research and interpretation are ever-changing, as they are intimately tied to democratic development. But, in a time of deepening democracy, the stories told in these museums and memorials satisfy the popular need to know and appreciate our common heritage.

Each of the peace museums scattered throughout Asia is unique, partly owing to specific local historical and social conditions. However, a searching reflection on history reveals that we all have a common concern for human rights and peace. They are our universal values, and they should inform every country's conduct. They also indicate important directions in museum design.

UNESCO, as with the non-governmental organization World Council of Peace Museums, has worked hard to advocate universal values and pacifism. Their efforts deserve our respect, and we can surely learn from them as we establish peace museums to commemorate our developmental experience, from colonial governance and authoritarian rule to full-fledged democracy.

Currently, Taiwan's most important peace museums are the Green Island Human Rights Memorial Park, which is already partly open to the public, and the Taipei 228 Memorial Museum, completed in 1997.

V1

Interior exhibits at the Green Island Human Rights Memorial Park

Interior exhibits at the Green Island Human Rights Memorial Park

# Green Island Human Rights Memorial Park

In 2000, Taiwan experienced the first democratic succession of political parties in its history. In December 2001, the first Human Rights Month of the twenty-first century, the popular exhibition "Road to Freedom: Retrospective on Taiwan's Democratic Struggle and Human Rights Movement" was held in the first-floor gallery of the Presidential Building, once an agency of oppression and violence. This exhibit was a success, attracting a lot of visitors.

On December 10, 2002, President Chen Shui-bian went to Green Island, which rivals the infamous Robbin Island, where opponents of apartheid such as Nelson Mandela were incarcerated. On the northeast corner of Green Island stands what was once a political prison. The presidential purpose behind this trip was to join its former inmates—the survivors—in pushing open the gate of the prison, symbolizing the end of injustice, and to inaugurate the first phase of the Green Island Human Rights Memorial Park.

The park is to commemorate Taiwan's political prisoner experience from 1951 to 1987, to bear witness to the history of the struggle for democracy and human rights, and to promote human rights education.

Green Island is a lone island located 33 kilometers off Taiwan's southeast coast. It has always been isolated from outside influence and has remained undeveloped, retaining its uniquely beautiful natural landscape. Once the ideal site for a political prison, now it is perfectly suited to ecological preservation.

Green Island was not always isolated from cultural

influence, as along the perimeter of the park there are still several prehistoric Austronesian sites awaiting the attention of archeologists. The planning of the park has touched on specific issues of history, culture, architecture, landscape, cultural preservation, museum management, tourism, ecology, and sustainable development. These various aspects give the park a complex yet charismatic personality that is sure to attract visitors.

## New Life Correction Center

The Green Island Human Rights Memorial Park incorporates the remnants of two overlapping political prisoner detention sites. These are the New Life Correction Center concentration camp (1951 to 1965) and the enclosed prison, Oasis Villa (1972 to 1987). The latter is already open to the public, but most of the buildings of the former have been destroyed. Why? We know Ma Ying-jeou as the current mayor of Taipei City, but from 1993 to 1996 he served as Minister of Justice. In his term of office, he demolished or reconstructed many sites that were crucially important during the White Terror in the 1950s and 1960s, to make way for a job training center for the repeat offenders held on Green Island. Only two buildings and a sixty-meter-long perimeter now remain of the camp.

Ma's move reflects a myopic ignorance, an official indifference to history. This is an irredeemable loss to the historical record and to the commemoration of victims of oppression. However, reconstruction is now in the planning stages for some of the major buildings, which will become spaces in which oral history, cultural artifacts and images join to evoke an important period in history.

## Oasis Villa

The only remaining prison on Green Island, Oasis Villa has all the charm of reinforced concrete. It is as plain and gloomy as a military barracks. The future plan for the facility stresses letting the atmosphere of the site remain as it has been, so that the visitor will be transported back in time. There is already a theater and an exhibition hall to tell the many amazing stories that weave through the walls at Oasis Villa.

V3

Interior exhibits at the Taipei 228 Memorial Museum

## The Future Development of the Park

Green Island boasts rich marine resources: in its waters are over 200 species of coral (including the world's largest single living coral), as well as more than 300 species of fish and 200 species of shellfish, eminently qualifying it as a national marine reserve. Every year, this sunny island attracts 350 thousand visitors, or four to five thousand daily during the peak summer period. Thus, the Green Island Human Rights Memorial Park, currently still in the planning stages, will become a welcome addition to an island environment that is already rich with life.

It is anticipated that the park and its surrounding area will offer a unique historical, cultural, and natural space. With their own eyes, visitors will see the political prison, prompting reflection on the value that the human race places on life. They will also take in the natural scenery and observe the marine ecology. This will be an intense and eye-opening experience for one and all.

# Memorials to the February 28 Incident and the White Terror

In the late 1980s, the Taiwanese people were breaking political taboos one after another. A positive outcome of this process has been increased reflection on and commemoration of major political incidents, such as the February 28 Incident and the White Terror. This new interest in the past has taken concrete form in various memorial buildings and monuments, the most widely known of which is the Taipei 228 Peace Park, host to the national 228 Memorial and the Taipei 228 Memorial Museum, the latter set up by Chen Shui-bian during his mayoralty (1994 to 1998).

There was no place untouched by the February 28 massacre, which also went by the name of "Countrywide Sweep." With many cities and counties having set up 228 memorials, the design and symbolic significance is different in each case: some tell of the search for love and peace, others stress the pursuit of truth, while still others express the hope of ethnic reconciliation.

There are also memorials or parks at important White Terror sites like Liuchangli and Racetrack in Taipei City, Luku Village in Taipei County. Besides, the government is preparing on legislative work to pave the way for the National Human Rights Museum, to be set up in Taipei. There have been suggestions for other museums, such as the office of the *Formosa Monthly*, which was involved in the 1979 Kaohsiung Incident, as well as the Taiwan Garrison Command's

V4

The Taipei 228 Memorial Museum by night

Martial Law Section Jail in Hsintien.

The Taipei 228 Memorial Museum was opened to the public on the fiftieth anniversary of the Incident. Its functions include exhibition, education, collection, and research, and it serves as a space for activities and for the storage of historical materials. As Taiwan's first peace museum to use a public ownership-private management model, there was a great deal of difficulty involved in operating it.

Memorial buildings are often squeezed on either side by contemporary political disputes. A case in point is Taiwan's first February 28 memorial, established in Chiayi City in 1989 in the midst of a confrontation between the local government and the Kuomintang, which at the time still controlled the central government. The Taipei 228 Memorial Museum, similarly, was embroiled in disputes over national and ethnic identity, ideology, and historical interpretation during its development process.

V5

The 228 Memorial in Taipei, set up by the central government

These disputes were tangential and arose because the project was a political football for the different parties. This kind of confrontation is a critical problem for politically polarized Taiwan. A major test of the wisdom of the Taiwanese people will be to discover how to let Taiwan's current and future peace museums stick to their original creative intentions and exercise their unique functions independent of successions in central or local government. Only by passing this test will Taiwan's peace museums do what they are supposed to do, which is to probe history and promote human rights education.

V6

Taiwan's first 228 memorial, located on Mituo Road, Chiayi City

| Established | Name | Place | Remarks | |
|---|---|---|---|---|
| 1976 | Freedom Cemetery | Taipei County | Final resting place for some of the democratic fighters in *Free China* magazine | |
| 1982 | Gikong Formosan Presbyterian Church | Taipei City | Originally the residence of Lin Yi-hsiung, place where his mother and daughters were murdered | |
| 1989 | Mituo Road 228 Memorial | Chiayi City | First memorial to 228 in Taiwan | |
| 1990 | Pao Chueh Temple Homeland Memorial for Departed Souls | Taichung City | To remember the some 30,000 Taiwanese soldiers who were drafted by the Japanese for World War Two | |
| 1992 | Pingtung County 228 Memorial | Pingtung | | |
| 1993 | Leshin Wadan Memorial Cemetery | Taoyuan | Final resting place of the Indigenous self-rule leader, whose statue is inside | |
| 1993 | Kaohsiung City 228 Memorial | Kaohsiung City | Near where the "Butcher of Kaohsiung" launched that city's 228 massacre | |
| 1993 | Patu Station 228 Memorial | Keelung | Built at the site of the tragedy (*see p. 102*) | |
| 1993 | Kaohsiung County 228 Memorial | Kangshan | | |
| 1994 | Linpien Township 228 Memorial | Pingtung | | |
| 1994 | Uyongu Yatauyungana (Kao Yi-sheng) Family Cemetery | Chiayi County | Grave of an Indigenous self-rule leader—not getting a gravestone until 1994 | |
| 1995 | 228 Memorial | Taipei City | Established by the central government | |
| 1995 | Taichung City 228 Memorial | Taichung City | | |
| 1995 | Tainan City 228 Memorial | Tainan City | | |
| 1996 | Taipei 228 Peace Park | Taipei City | Location of the 228 Memorial and the Taipei 228 Memorial Museum | |
| 1996 | Mt. Ali 228 Memorial | Chiayi County | Commemorating Indigenous martyrs in the Incident | |
| 1996 | Chiayi 228 Memorial Museum | Chiayi City | Taiwan's first 228 Memorial Museum | |
| 1996 | Chiayi City 228 Memorial Park | Chiayi City | First 228 memorial park in Taiwan, contains a new memorial plaque | ❶ |
| 1996 | Tainan County 228 Memorial | Hsinying | | |
| 1997 | Taipei 228 Memorial Museum | Taipei City | Site of the radio station that broadcast news of the Incident throughout the island in 1947 | ❷ |
| 1997 | Hualien County 228 Memorial | Hualien | | |
| 1998 | 228 Incident Starting Point Memorial | Taipei City | Where the first shots were fired by the KMT on February 27, 1947 | |
| 1998 | Dr. Chen Wen-chen Memorial Room | Taipei City | Commemorating the sacrifice of an overseas scholar in the US who died defending democracy and human rights | ❸ |
| 1998 | Democratic Heroes Park | Miaoli | Contains Taiwan's first memorial dedicated to victims of the White Terror | |
| 1998 | Tang Teh-chang Memorial Park | Tainan City | Remembering a respected human rights lawyer, whose statue is inside | |
| 1999 | Cheng Nan-jung Memorial Museum | Taipei City | Former offices of *Freedom Era* magazine, where Cheng set himself afire in his fight for freedom of speech | ❹ |
| 1999 | Taoyuan County 228 Memorial | Taoyuan | | |
| 1999 | Green Island Human Rights Monument | Green Island | At present, just one part of the Green Island Human Rights Memorial Park | |
| 2000 | Luku Incident Memorial Park | Taipei County | Contains a memorial plaque | |
| 2000 | Kukeng 228 Memorial | Yunlin | Buried remains of people's militia martyrs discovered here | |
| 2001 | Chingyi University 228 Memorial | Taichung County | The only 228 memorial located on a university campus | |
| 2001 | Juan Chao-jih 228 Memorial Museum | Pingtung | A tribute to 228 martyr Juan Chao-jih, the first privately established 228 memorial museum | ❺ |
| 2001 | Keelung City 228 Memorial | Keelung | | |
| 2001 | Tali City 228 Memorial | Taichung County | | |
| 2002 | Racetrack Memorial Park | Taipei City | At least several thousand killed during the White Terror on these execution grounds | |
| 2002 | Taipei County 228 Memorial | Sanchung | | |
| 2002 | Cheng Nan-jung Memorial Cemetery | Taipei County | Cheng's final resting place, with his statue inside | |
| 2002 | Taiwan Democratic Movement Museum | Ilan | Archiving historical materials covering 100 years of the opposition and democratic movements | ❻ |
| 2002 | Green Island Human Rights Memorial Park | Green Island | Under contruction on the site of New Life Correction Center; part of Oasis Villa is now open to the public | ❼ |
| 2003 | Li Wan-chu Memorial Museum | Yunlin | Old residence of this pioneer in Taiwan's democratic movement | |
| 2003 | Liuchangli Memorial Park | Taipei City | Near a public cemetery where many political prisoners were buried | |
| 2004 | Wunyulan Battle Momument | Nantou | In Puli, the site of clash between students' militia and butcher squads in the 228 Incident | |
| 1800s | Liao Wen-yi Family Cemetery | Yunlin | Final resting place for a family that had big role in early movement for Taiwan Independence | |
| being planned | Kaohsiung Incident starting point | Kaohsiung City | Starting point a traffic circle, had far-reaching influence on Taiwan's later historical development | |
| being planned | National Human Rights Memorial Museum | Taipei City | Legislation currently being pursued | |

Telephone: ❶ +886-52-759-038  ❷ +886-2-2389-7228  ❸ +886-2-2363-3703  ❹ +886-2-2546-8766  ❺ +886-8-875-1694  ❻ +886-3-965-0515  ❼ +886-89-671-095

2

5

6

10

11

3

4

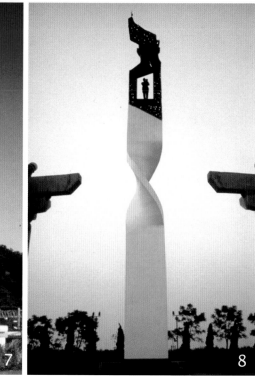

7

8

1. Dr. Chen Wen-chen Memorial Room

2. Racetrack Memorial Park

3. Taiwan Democratic Movement Museum

4. Green Island Human Rights Memorial Park

5. Pingtung County 228 Memorial

6. The Second Memorial Plaque in Chiayi City

7. Patu Station 228 Memorial

8. Tainan County 228 Memorial

9. Kaohsiung City 228 Memorial

10. Tainan City 228 Memorial

11. Liuchangli Memorial Park

12. Taichung City 228 Memorial

13. Kaohsiung County 228 Memorial

14. Cheng Nan-jung Memorial Museum

9

12

13

14

# Credits

### We would especially like to thank the following for providing information and other support.

Chang Yen-hsien 張炎憲
Chen Chien-ting 陳建廷
Chen Feng-hua 陳鳳華
Chen Yi-shen 陳儀深
Chiang Tien-lu 姜天陸
Hsieh Tsung-min 謝聰敏
Hsu Chin-fa 許進發
Hsu Fang-ting 許芳庭
Huang Hsien-tung 黃憲東
Huang Hua 黃華
Rev. Hsu Cheng-tao 許承道牧師
Rev. Kao Chun-ming 高俊明牧師
Shen Huai-yu 沈懷玉

Tsai Tsai-yuan 蔡財源
Tsai Yi-ta 蔡易達
Central News Agency 中央通訊社
Chilin Foundation 慈林教育基金會
Fifties White Terror Political Cases Redress Promotion
    Association 五十年代白色恐怖案件平反促進會
Formosan Political Prisoner Association 台灣政治受難者
    關懷協會
Gikong Presbyterian Church 義光教會
Ministry of Justice 法務部
Overseas Chinese Affairs Commission 僑務委員會
Yu-Li Hospital, Department of Health, Executive Yuan
    衛生署玉里醫院

# Index

# 人權之路 台灣民主人權回顧

| | |
|---|---|
| 企劃・出版 | 財團法人陳文成博士紀念基金會（台灣） |
| 顧問 | 李筱峰・陳銘城・楊碧川・盧兆麟・薛化元 |
| 主編 | 李禎祥 |
| 編撰 | 李禎祥・林世煜・曹欽榮・胡慧玲・鄭純宜・林芳微 |
| 翻譯 | Lynn Miles (pp. 25-32, 34-51, 74-98, 100-138, 152-160, 169-173) |
| | Darryl Sterk (pp. 4-24, 33, 52-73, 99, 139, 161, 164-168) |
| | 鄭純宜 (pp. 140-151, 162-163) |
| 審校 | 林世煜・滕兆鏘・Lynn Miles・Darryl Sterk・鄭純宜 |
| 封面・美術設計 | 林書毓 |

**財團法人陳文成博士紀念基金會**

106台北市新生南路3段25巷1號2樓
電話：02-2363-3703
傳真：02-2366-1468
cwc1950@ms72.hinet.net
郵政劃撥14267676 財團法人陳文成博士紀念基金會
著作權顧問：詹文凱律師
法律顧問：李勝雄律師

| | |
|---|---|
| 製版印刷 | 海王印刷事業股份有限公司 |
| | 235台北縣中和市中正路800號11樓之2 |

初版一刷：2004年12月
定價：新台幣900元・美金40元
版權所有・翻印必究
ISBN：986-80776-0-5

| | |
|---|---|
| 贊助指導 | 行政院文化建設委員會　http://www.cca.gov.tw |
| | 陳文成教授基金會（美國） |

# The Road to Freedom
## Taiwan's Postwar Human Rights Movement

| | |
|---|---|
| **Planning and Publishing** | Dr. Chen Wen-chen Memorial Foundation (Taiwan) |
| **Advisors** | Lee Shiao-feng, Chen Ming-chen, Yang Pi-chuan, Lu Chao-lin, Hsueh Hua-yuan |
| **Editor** | Lee Chen-hsiang |
| **Editorial Writers** | Lee Chen-hsiang, Lin Shih-yu, Ronald C. J. Tsao, Hu Hui-lin, Cheng Tsun-i, Lin Hong-vi |
| **Translators** | Lynn Miles (pp. 25-32, 34-51, 74-98, 100-138, 152-160, 169-173) |
| | Darryl Sterk (pp. 4-24, 33, 52-73, 99, 139, 161, 164-168) |
| | Cheng Tsun-i (pp. 140-151, 162-163) |
| **Manuscript Review** | Lin Shih-yu, Terng Chao-chiang, Lynn Miles, Darryl Sterk, Cheng Tsun-i |
| **Graphic Design & Cover** | Lin Shu-yu |

**Dr. Chen Wen-chen Memorial Foundation**

2nd Floor, No. 1, Lane 25, Hsinsheng South Road, Section 3, 106 Taipei Taiwan

Tel: +886-2-2363-3703   Fax: +886-2-2366-1468   cwc1950@ms72.hinet.net

Postal Account: 14267676  Dr. Chen Wen-chen Memorial Foundation

Copyright Advisor: Attorney Chan Wen-kai

Legal Advisor: Attorney Li Sheng-hsiung

| | |
|---|---|
| **Printing** | Haiwang Printing Company |
| | No. 800 Chungcheng Road 11-2, Jhongho, Taipei County 235 Taiwan |

First Edition: December 2004

Price: NT$900 (US$40)

©2004 All Rights Reserved

ISBN:986-80776-0-5

| | |
|---|---|
| **Financial Assistance** | Council for Cultural Affairs, Executive Yuan   http://www.cca.gov.tw |
| | Prof. Chen Wen-chen Memorial Foundation (U.S.) |